A FOUNTAIN OF GARDENS

Plants and Herbs of the Bible

A FOUNTAIN OF GARDENS

Plants and Herbs of the Bible

WILMA PATERSON

MAINSTREAM
PUBLISHING

Copyright © Wilma Paterson, 1990
All rights reserved
First published in Great Britain 1990 by
MAINSTREAM PUBLISHING COMPANY (EDINBURGH) LTD
7 Albany Street
Edinburgh EH1 3UG
ISBN 1 85158 255 X (cloth)

British Library Cataloguing in Publication Data
Paterson, Wilma
A fountain of gardens
1. Bible. Special subjects: Plants
I. Title
220.8'581

ISBN 1-85158-255-X

Typeset in 12 on 13 pt Bodoni by
C. R. Barber & Partners (Highlands) Ltd, Fort William, Scotland
Printed in Spain by Cayfosa, Barcelona

For my mother

A garden inclosed is my sister, my spouse; a spring shut up, a fountain sealed. Thy plants are an orchard of pomegranates, with pleasant fruits; camphire, with spikenard. Spikenard and saffron; calamus and cinnamon, with all trees of frankincense; myrrh and aloes, with all the chief spices: A fountain of gardens, a well of living waters, and streams from Lebanon. Awake, O north wind; and come, thou south; blow upon my garden, that the spices thereof may flow out. Let my beloved come into his garden, and eat his pleasant fruits.

(SONG OF SOLOMON 4: 12–16)

ACKNOWLEDGEMENTS

The author and publishers would like to thank Dr Robert Mill of the Royal Botanic Garden, Edinburgh, for his expertise and attention to detail. Thanks are also extended to the staff of Glasgow University Library, especially of the Special Collections and to Mr Bill Angell for his photographic contributions and also to Maeve Hek for typing the manuscript.

INTRODUCTION

The natural history of the Bible, and in particular its botany, has fascinated scholars and ordinary readers for many hundreds of years, and while an understanding and knowledge of the plants is often important in clarifying the meaning of obscure and difficult passages in the highly figurative language, with its many similes and metaphors, an awareness of the characteristics of the plants also helps to give an insight into the everyday world of the Scriptures—domestic life, commerce and agriculture, religious observance, the exotic, the erotic and the intricacies of class, family and other relationships. Bible society was essentially agrarian, towns were small, and people lived close to the land. So they were necessarily aware of the properties and culture of the plants around them, which provided their food, fuel, shelter, clothing and medicine. Bread, the staff of life then, as today, was the mainstay of the diet of ancient Israel, so the crops which provided it are frequently mentioned in the Bible, both literally and metaphorically. Wheat and barley were the main ones, and with grapes, olives, figs, dates and pomegranates, they made up the 'seven species' with which the Land of Israel was blessed. Apart from fruit trees and flowers, gardens provided pulses (chick peas, lentils, broad beans), leeks, onions, garlic, melons and herbs for flavouring such as coriander, cummin, dill, mint and oregano, while many pot herbs were collected in the wild. The *bitter herbs* of EXODUS 12: 8 which the Jews were instructed to eat with their Passover probably included the wild chicory, lettuce and dandelion-type plants which are still eaten as salad in the Holy Land. Plants played an important part in religious worship too—ancient trees for example were revered and almost deified—and for the various festivals such as Passover, Pentecost and Tabernacles the first fruits of the harvest were offered, and there were strict religious laws which had to be observed concerning this—which extended even to the rights of the gleaning of the fields by the poor. Incense was needed during religious ceremony, as much as anything to help counteract the various disagreeable smells that must have arisen from the slaughtering of animals, sprinkling of blood and burning of flesh. The ingredients for incense and holy anointing oils came mainly from expensive and exotic imported gums and resins, roots and barks. Incense, oils and cosmetics also had their place in the secular world of the rich, of the poet and the prostitute. Frankincense was chewed to sweeten the breath, it was burnt and the ash used to make *kohl* for painting the eyes, while perfumes were used to mask body odours (particularly of the feet) and to sprinkle on clothes, couches and beds.

Flowers were enjoyed for their fragrance and for decoration, and many plants were used medicinally and superstitiously, though any therapeutic or magical properties are not, of course, highlighted in the Bible, which is concerned with God's superior, divine and all-embracing powers. So Rachel's superstitious belief in the fertility-inducing properties of the mandrake is not rewarded, and she does not conceive until the Lord sees fit to give her a child.

> *Lo, children are an heritage of the Lord:*
> *and the fruit of the womb is his reward*
>
> (PSALMS 127: 3)

I make no apology for taking my Scripture quotations from the *Authorised Version* of King James VI, which is now so sadly neglected in our churches and schools everywhere, although I have naturally referred to others more accurate, which are based on a sounder knowledge of the Holy Land and its botany. There is not in my opinion a recent translation of the Bible which even *approaches* the *Authorised Version* for the evocative powers and beauty of the language, and of the poetry, much of which has been absorbed into the English language over the centuries. There are naturally many inaccuracies—

European names such as box, hazel or chestnut for instance were given to many Bible plants simply because they were familiar to the reader. I have corrected the accepted discrepancies, but it is beyond the scope or intention of this little book to present the minutiae of scholarly argument over some of the more intricate questions of plant identification, some of which are unlikely *ever* to be resolved. I have consulted the writings of the early travellers and botanists and recent researches of scholars working in the Holy Land, and I have dealt with all the important plants of the *Old Testament* (which was written mainly in Hebrew, with some Aramaic, after more than 1,000 years of oral transmission) and of the *New Testament* which was written in Greek. There are plant references in the books known as the *Apocrypha*, but I have omitted these, as they do not form part of the Hebrew canon because of their secular nature.

I hope that this book will interest those to whom the Scriptures are important for religious reasons, those who relish the rich imagery and language of the Bible, those who enjoy plantlore and plants and finding new uses for them, and those who get pleasure from that picture of a bygone age which the Bible and its plants so vividly portray.

Wilma Paterson
July 1990

CONTENTS

ALMOND

Amygdalus communis

Moreover the word of the LORD came unto me, saying, Jeremiah, what seest thou? And I said, I see a rod of an almond tree.
Then said the Lord unto me, Thou hast well seen: for I will hasten my word to perform it.

(JEREMIAH 1: 11–12)

In other words, as the almond tree hastens to bud, so God makes haste to carry out his purpose. And in the Near East, where it is a native of Palestine and Syria, the almond is the first of all the fruit trees to blossom, its pink-white flowers appearing in late winter before the leaves. The blossom is an important artistic feature of the seven-branched candlestick of the Tabernacle (EXODUS 25: 31–35) and Aaron's rod which blossomed and bore fruit overnight, ensuring him the priesthood, was a branch of almond.

And it came to pass, that on the morrow Moses went into the tabernacle of witness; and, behold, the rod of Aaron for the house of Levi was budded, and brought forth buds, and bloomed blossoms, and yielded almonds.

(NUMBERS 17: 8)

Although a native of hot countries the almond has long been grown in Britain, 'We have them in our London gardens and orchards in good plentie,' wrote Gerard in 1597, though of course they were cultivated for their ornamental and early flowering qualities rather than for their fruit, which would be much inferior to the imported almonds. The Romans imported them and they have been used extensively in this country for centuries—prodigiously in the Middle Ages; the Royal Household of 1286 consumed the astonishing quantity of 28,500 lbs. They were used in many ways, added to dishes whole, blanched, fried, scattered on pottages and frequently pounded in a mortar and used as a thickening agent or to make marchpane or marzipan for sweetmeats.

Almond milk was used for sweet and savoury dishes and the upper classes consumed it as a substitute for cow's milk on fasting days.

Take fair almonds and blanch them and grind them with sugar water into fair milk . . . over and besides that it nourisheth, and is good for those that are troubled with the laske and bloodie flixe, it is profitable for those that have the pleurisie, and spet up filthie matter . . .

(*Gerard's* HERBALL *1597*)

Today we are less concerned with their medicinal qualities than their delicious flavour and their nutritive value—they are a useful diabetic food, made into cakes or biscuits, as they contain almost no starch. And they still occupy a special place in our lives as they did in Biblical times when Jacob instructed Judah to send them as a gift to Joseph when he was governor of Egypt.

. . . take of the best fruits in the land in your vessels, and carry down the man a present, a little balm, and a little honey, spices, and myrrh, nuts, and almonds.

(GENESIS 43: 11)

In present-day Israel they are part of the traditional *Kibbet* (Hebrew for treat) served to visitors along with dates, figs and raisins, and throughout Europe they are associated with festive occasions—christenings, weddings, Easter and Christmas—when special cakes, puddings, sweets and biscuits are prepared. The oil from almonds is valued today as well, both medicinally and by the cosmetic industry. Gerard [*1633*] is more reliable there than when discussing midwifery!

It is good for women that are newly delivered; for it quickly removeth the throwes which remain after their delivery. The oyle of almonds *do make smooth the hands and face of delicate persons, and clenseth the skin from all spots, pimples and lentils.*

It's good and nourishing too for old violins and as a lubricant for the delicate mechanisms of watches.

Almond blossom, representing the white hair of old age, appears in the wonderful last chapter of ECCLESIASTES:

. . . and the almond *tree shall flourish, and the grasshopper shall be a burden, and desire shall fail: because man goeth to his long home, and the mourners go about the streets:*

(ECCLESIASTES 12: 5)

The tree is well worth cultivating for these early delicate blossoms, and will thrive in ordinary well-drained soil and in town gardens. It's a valuable bee plant too, and can be a good source of nectar and pollen after the long winter months of confinement.

ALMOND PETIT FOURS
(Traditional recipe)

*Mix together equal quantities of ground
almonds and icing sugar with orange blossom
water to form a stiff paste. Form into little balls
and decorate with almonds or pistachio nuts.
Serve after dinner with coffee.*

Amygdalus incana

(ROSE FAMILY—*ROSACEAE*)

ALMUG THYINE EBONY

Pterocarpus santalinus Tetraclinis articulata   Diospyros ebenum

And the King made of the almug trees, pillars for the house of the Lord, and for the King's house, harps also and psalteries for singers: there came no such almug trees, nor were seen unto this day.

(1 KINGS 10: 12)

Although not linguistically certain, it's most probable that the almug is the red saunders or red sandalwood, a native of India and Sri Lanka.

And she gave the King an hundred and twenty talents of gold, and of spices great abundance, and precious stones: neither was there any such spice as the Queen of Sheba gave Solomon. And the servants also of Huram, and the servants of Solomon, which brought gold from Ophir, brought algum trees and precious stones.

(2 CHRONICLES 9: 9–10)

So the almug was clearly a prized commodity—and so it is to this day,—it appears in the BRITISH PHARMACEUTICAL CODEX. The biblical scholar Moldenke claims that red saunders is still used today for the manufacture of lyres and other musical instruments. In medieval Britain it was used as a colouring agent, and in the complex meat jellies which were a speciality of Norman cookery. It was also used to colour early gingerbreads and fashionable pottages:

And if thou will change the colour
take sanders and saffron,
and make the pottage sanguine colour
for winter season.

Medieval Norman recipe[1]

Saunders and alkanet (*Alkanna tinctoria*) were eventually replaced by cochineal, the dried bodies of an insect found on a particular cactus of Mexico, but that was well into the seventeenth century.

There are two other precious woods mentioned in the Bible. Thyine is a fragrant wood, producing a resin which was used for incense, from the thya tree, *Tetraclinis articulata*.

The merchandise of gold, and silver, and precious stones, and of pearls, and fine linen, and purple, and silk, and scarlet, and all thyine wood . . .

(REVELATION 18: 12)

The other is Ebony (*Diospyros ebenum*).

The men of Dedan were thy merchants; many isles were the merchandise of thine hand: they brought thee for a present horns of ivory and ebony.

(EZEKIEL 27: 15)

In the west, the mystique of the precious wood ebony is instilled in the nursery with the story of Snow White, whose hair was 'black as ebony' and whose skin was 'whiter than

16

snow'. And ebony is still the exotic commodity today that it must have been in the days of the prophet Ezekiel.

It was a luxury import from India and Sri Lanka, the heartwood of a tall evergreen tree, which in maturity becomes black. Hard and heavy, it can take a fine polish and it was prized for making instruments, ornaments and cabinets. This is the only mention of the wood in the Bible with another precious import—ivory, with which it was probably worked as an inlay, forming a strikingly beautiful contrast.

Various tropical and subtropical species of the genus *Diospyros* apart from *Diospyros ebenum* have provided ebony, and other woods have been stained in imitation of the genuine article. Favourite articles are brushes and mirrors and boxes.

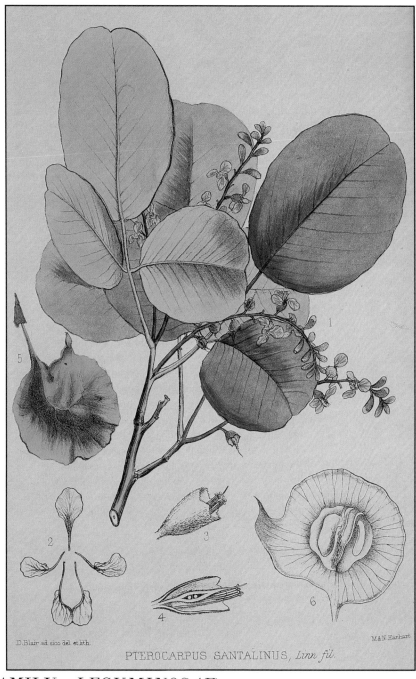

PTEROCARPUS SANTALINUS, *Linn fil.*

(PEA FAMILY—*LEGUMINOSAE*)

(CYPRESS FAMILY—*CUPRESSACEAE*)

(EBONY FAMILY—*EBENACEAE*)

17

LIGN-ALOE

Aquilaria agallocha

ALOE

Aloe vera

And there came also Nicodemus, which at the first came to Jesus by night, and brought a mixture of myrrh and aloes, *about an hundred pound weight. Then took they the body of Jesus, and wound it in linen clothes with the spices, as the manner of the Jews is to bury.*

(JOHN 19: 39–40)

You might think 100 pounds of embalming matter somewhat excessive for one body, and indeed some scholars have suggested that the true figure ought to be ten, but whatever the quantity (and Josephus recorded 500 spice bearers at Herod's funeral) it's almost certain that the substance mixed with myrrh was the bitter aloes used by the ancient Egyptians in embalming, and which is extracted from the leaves of *Aloe vera* and other species.

The plant has some religious significance in the Middle East. Muslims hang it up over their doorways as a protection against evil in the same way as elder and rowan were used in Europe. Here is Edward William Lane writing in his ACCOUNT OF THE MANNERS AND CUSTOMS OF THE MODERN EGYPTIANS in the 1830s.

It is a very common custom in Cairo to hang an aloe *plant over the door of a house; particularly over that of a new house, or over a door newly built: and this is regarded as a charm to insure long and flourishing lives to the inmates and long continuance to the house itself. The women also believe that the Prophet visits the house where this plant is suspended. The* aloe *thus hung without earth or water, will live for several years, and even blossom.*

The aloe is a succulent plant of the lily family, and to obtain the juice the leaves are cut off close to the stem and drained. It is then concentrated by evaporation or boiling and is poured into containers where it solidifies. Gerard, in 1597, mentions it being imported to England in skins. It was known then, and now, mainly as a safe and effective purgative (now particularly in veterinary medicine) though Culpeper suggests mixing it with oil of roses and vinegar and applying it to the forehead and temples to ease headaches. Nowadays it is still used occasionally for painting the nails of persistent biters, though my mother's remedy for weaning a reluctant infant by anointing the nipples with bitter aloes is certainly a thing of the past. Extract of *Aloe vera* however is used in fashionable cosmetics—shampoos, soaps and face creams. In PROVERBS 7: 16–17, 'aloes' means something quite different. This is the temptress/harlot speaking:

I have decked my bed with coverings of tapestry, with carved works, with fine linen of Egypt.
I have perfumed my bed with myrrh, aloes *and cinnamon.*

Aloes, in this case, refers to the precious aromatic heart of the *lign-aloe* or eaglewood tree of India, which was used for perfuming clothes and apartments, for incense and sometimes also as a cordial in fainting or epileptic fits. The pieces of wood were kept in pewter boxes to prevent them drying out, and then ground on marble and added to whatever liquids suited the purpose.

God, thy God, hath anointed thee with the oil of gladness above thy fellows. All thy garments smell of myrrh, and aloes, *and cassia, out of the ivory palaces, whereby they have made thee glad.*

(PSALMS 45: 7–8)

Aloe vulgaris

(LILY FAMILY—*LILIACEAE*)

(EAGLEWOOD—*THYMELAEACEAE*)

19

ANISE

Pimpinella anisum

DILL

Anethum graveolens

Woe unto you, scribes and Pharisees, hypocrites! for ye pay tithe of mint and anise *and cummin, and have omitted the weightier matters of the law, judgment, mercy, and faith: these ought ye to have done, and not to leave the other undone.*

(MATTHEW 23: 23)

This is the only mention of anise in the Bible—where the Pharisees are accused of concentrating on minor issues while neglecting important ones—but it is now generally accepted that it is a mistranslation and the plant in question is really dill. There are however similarities in these two plants and both have been widely used for their carminative properties. Here is Gerard on anise.

The seed wasteth and consumeth winde, and is good against belchings and upbraidings of the stomacke, alaieth gripings of the belly, provoketh urine gently, maketh abundance of milke, and stirreth up bodily lust . . .

(*Gerard's* HERBALL, 1597)

And this may indeed be as true as his assertion (1597) that aniseed *Being chewed it maketh the breath sweete.* (Those old schoolday favourites, aniseed balls, are certainly good for this).

Anise is a native of the Middle East, but has long been cultivated, and was grown in medieval English herb gardens—though such was the demand for the seeds that they were imported as well. They were used to flavour cakes and biscuits, to help digestion after large meals and for liqueurs like the French anisette. In Spain the Basques make a liqueur with sloes and anise called Patxaran—a little like our sloe gin.

Dill seed was similarly believed to alleviate 'gripings and windinesse' and to increase the milk in nurses. The leaves can be used as well as the seeds. Chop them finely and add to white sauces, creamed potatoes, salads and soups. Dill is excellent too, with chicken and fish. It's an easy herb to grow. Sow the seed in spring, thin out leaving eight to ten inches between the plants and keep free of weeds. The plants grow to about three feet. When the seeds are ripening, pick off the heads and lay them on sheets of paper to dry. Store the seeds in air-tight containers and use to make dill tea (1 tsp. seeds boiled in a pint of water for 15 minutes, strained and sweetened with honey) for flatulence.

Try pickling cucumbers with dill seeds and sprigs of the fresh herb. This is popular in Germany and Scandinavia, and in a less sweet form in the Middle East.

If you like aniseed-flavoured liqueurs the following recipe is simple and worth making.

ANISEED LIQUEUR
(Italian recipe)

1 litre (1¾ pt) alcohol (90 per cent)
50 g (2 oz) green aniseed
5 g (¼oz) coriander, cinnamon and cloves,
zest of half an orange,
a piece of vanilla pod
1 litre (1¾ pt) water
1.5 kg (2½ lb) sugar

Put the alcohol in a Kilner jar with the flavourings and leave to macerate for three weeks. Make a syrup with the sugar and water, allow to cool and add to the alcohol mixture. Mix well, leave for an hour then filter. Keep the liqueur in tightly-sealed bottles.

(CARROT FAMILY—*UMBELLIFERAE*)

APPLE

Malus sylvestris

Although it is commonly believed that the apple was the forbidden fruit of the Garden of Eden—an idea that has been reinforced throughout the history of painting and literature—in fact neither the name of the fruit nor the tree is mentioned in the text, and we are left wondering. Apple (tree or fruit) *is* mentioned, however, several times in the Old Testament and this translation of the Hebrew *tappuaḥ* has since been the subject of much debate—mainly because the apple at its best is a fruit of temperate countries and it was believed that it didn't grow in Biblical lands. So the citron, apricot, orange and quince have all been suggested as the tree and fruit which is celebrated in the SONG OF SOLOMON:

> *As the* apple *tree among the trees of the wood, so is my beloved among the sons. I sat down under his shadow with great delight, and his fruit was sweet to my taste.*
>
> (SONG OF SOLOMON 2: 3)

But linguistically apple is sounder and it's also referred to in ancient Egyptian papyri of the period of Ramses II (1298–1235 B.C.) and in Pliny's HISTORIA NATURALIS of the 1st century A.D. (He refers to both red and white Syrian apples). Much sweeter than our northern varieties, and perhaps insipid to our tastes, Middle-Eastern apples do have a delicious aroma and it's for this that they are most prized there. They are offered to visitors to smell, to sick children or people suffering from sea-sickness or faintness and often placed above the neck of a water pitcher to scent the water.

> *Stay me with flagons, comfort me with* apples: *for I am sick of love.*
>
> (SONG OF SOLOMON 2: 5)
>
> *. . . thy breasts shall be as clusters of the vine, and the smell of thy nose like* apples.
>
> (SONG OF SOLOMON 7: 8)

The most naturally appealing of fruits, apples are delicious, attractive and seductive (Snow White is tempted by a rosy but poisoned apple) and children love them. They have been popular in Britain since Roman times when several new varieties were introduced and developed, but, of the earliest named apples, one was the pearmain (around 1200) and another the costard which was popular from the 13th to 17th centuries. (A costermonger was the person who sold these, though later his wares extended to other fruits and vegetables). In 1629 John Parkinson named 57 kinds of apple—pippins, pomewaters, bittersweets, blanderelles—and though we are now reduced to a mere handful we continue to enjoy them in many and varied forms—not least in their fermented state!

Cider-making came from Normandy to Kent and Sussex in the 12th century and quickly spread to other parts of the country (wine of pearmains is recorded as a part-payment of rent in Norfolk) and apple tarts and pies have been popular since medieval times, flavoured with cloves and cinnamon and sometimes mixed with pork and other meats. Medicinally the fruit is valued for its malic and tartaric acids and its digestive properties.

Gerard recommends the juice 'for the tempering of melancholy humours' and an ointment, called 'Pomatum,' 'with the pulpe of Apples and Swines grease and Rose water, which is used to beautifie the face, and to take away the roughnes of the skin'.

Apple trees are very popular and the beautiful blossoms a delight to bees—the nectar producing a lovely light-amber honey. This was used with apples and almond milk to make the old English pottage *appulmos* which would be prettily decorated with apple blossom in April and May. Here's an Elizabethan recipe for:

APPLE TART

You must boil your apples in fair water, and when they be boiled enough, put them in a bowl, and bruise them with a ladle, and when they be cold, strain them; and put in red wine or claret wine, and so season it with sugar, cinnamon and ginger.

(This is the filling of course. You need also a pastry case of puff or shortcrust pastry).[2]

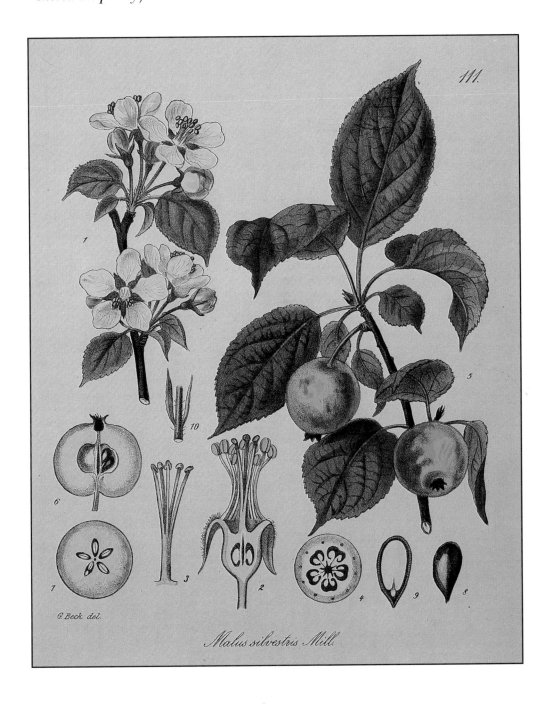

G. Beck del.

Malus silvestris Mill.

(ROSE FAMILY—*ROSACEAE*)

BALM

Commiphora gileadensis

STORAX

Liquidambar orientalis

And they sat down to eat bread: and they lifted up their eyes and looked, and, behold, a company of Ishmeelites came from Gilead with their camels bearing spicery and balm *and myrrh, going to carry it down to Egypt.*

(GENESIS 37: 25)

Balm here refers to the storax tree about which Gerard writes in 1597,

Of this gum there are made sundry excellent perfumes, pomanders, sweete waters, sweete bags, and sweete washing bals, and divers other sweete chaines and bracelets . . .

The Bible, particularly the SONG OF SOLOMON, is full of references to perfumes, oils and ointments. Cosmetics and incenses flourished in Assyria and Sumeria, and the sensual pleasures of fragrances and their aphrodisiac qualities are celebrated in the poetry of the period. Perfumes were an indispensable part of the toilet of the rich, and odoriferous plants were cultivated from very early times: the hanging gardens of Babylon, for instance, were renowned for their fragrance and there was a brisk foreign trade in exotic gums and resins.

The balsam tree of Judea (*Commiphora gileadensis*), with its many mystical associations is referred to in the *Old Testament* as 'spice':

I am come into my garden, my sister, my spouse: I have gathered my myrrh with my spice; *I have eaten my honeycomb with my honey; I have drunk my wine with my milk: eat, O friends; drink, yea, drink abundantly, O beloved.*

(SONG OF SOLOMON 5: 1)

This desert shrub, or small tree, was probably one of the gifts which the Queen of Sheba brought to King Solomon from Arabia and its resin was greatly prized—as an ingredient of holy oil and perfume and as an important healing agent for wounds and snake bites: 'The marvellous effects that it worketh in new and greene wounds, were heere too long to set downe . . .' says Gerard, and its healing properties are mentioned in the Bible too—

Is there no balm *in Gilead; is there no physician there? why then is not the health of the daughter of my people recovered?*

(JEREMIAH 8: 22)

Balm of Gilead, with its evocative and magical name, is rarely used medicinally now, but in the 16th century it certainly was:

Naturall Balsame taken in a morning fasting, with a little Rose water or wine, to the quantitie of five or six drops, helpeth those that be asthmatike, or short of winde: it prevaileth against the pains of the bladder, and stomack, and comforteth the same mightily.

(*Gerard's* HERBALL, 1597)

24

The popular lemon balm, sweet balm or bee-balm as it is known by bee-keepers is quite different. *Melissa officinalis* is a common and easily-grown garden plant of the mint family, which like borage was a well-known remedy for melancholy in the 16th and 17th centuries. It has a fragrant lemon smell and taste and you can make a pleasant tea with the leaves. This is cooling in cases of colds and flu or mild fevers.

LIQUIDAMBAR ORIENTALIS, *Mill.*

M & N Hanhart, imp.

(FRANKINCENSE FAMILY—*BURSERACEAE*)

(WITCH-HAZEL FAMILY—*HAMAMELIDACEAE*)

BARLEY
Hordeum vulgare

And I heard a voice in the midst of the four beasts say, A measure of wheat for a penny, and three measures of barley for a penny; and see thou hurt not the oil and the wine.

(REVELATION 6: 6)

Barley, probably man's most ancient aliment, is frequently mentioned in the Bible—usually with wheat, to which it is, as here, considered inferior—the food of poor people or animals. The five loaves which were miraculously increased to feed the multitude of 5,000 were made of barley:

There is a lad here, which hath five barley loaves, and two small fishes: but what are they among so many?

(JOHN 6: 9)

and Elisha received a present of 20 barley loaves.

And there came a man from Baal-shalisha, and brought the man of God bread of the firstfruits, twenty loaves of barley, and full ears of corn in the husk thereof. And he said, Give unto the people, that they may eat. And his servitor said, What, should I set this before an hundred men? He said again, Give the people, that they may eat: for thus saith the LORD, They shall eat, and shall leave thereof. So he set it before them, and they did eat, and left thereof, according to the word of the LORD.

(2 KINGS 4: 42–44)

Barley requires less good soil than wheat, and also less time to mature, so it would be ready to offer at the feast of the Passover. But because of its meaner status it figures also in the bizarre 'jealousy offering' of NUMBERS 5: 15:

Then shall the man bring his wife unto the priest, and he shall bring her offering for her, the tenth part of an ephah of barley meal; he shall pour no oil upon it, nor put frankincense thereon; for it is an offering of jealousy, an offering of memorial, bringing iniquity to remembrance.

Here if a husband suspects his wife of infidelity (and he doesn't even have to have *grounds* for the suspicion!) he has to bring her to the priest with the offering and she is subjected to a weird and horrifying ritual which will ultimately prove her guilt or innocence. If guilty she will suffer miscarriage and if innocent she will bear a child. Stern stuff this . . .

And when he (the priest) hath made her to drink the water, then it shall come to pass, that, if she be defiled, and have done trespass against her husband, that the water that causeth the curse shall enter into her, and become bitter, and her belly shall swell, and her thigh shall rot: and the woman shall

*be a curse among her people. And if the woman be not defiled, but be clean;
then she shall be free, and shall conceive seed.*

(NUMBERS 5: 27–28)

Barley has a more homely image these days, especially in Scotland as the basic ingredient
of Scotch broth, that marvellous soup of leeks, carrots, peas, etc. about which even tetchy Dr
Johnson had a good word after a first sampling, 'I don't care how soon I eat it again!' Barley
in bannock form was the daily bread of Scotland's Highlands and Islands before wheat
loaves made with yeast arrived there. Now its real importance is confined to the whisky
industry, malted barley being the basis of the sublime malt whiskies of Scotland, and of beer
too.

(GRASS FAMILY—*GRAMINEAE*)

27

BAY

Laurus nobilis

I have seen the wicked in great power, and spreading himself like a green bay tree. Yet he passed away, and, lo, he was not: yea, I sought him, but he could not be found.

(PSALMS 37: 35–36)

Although there is linguistic confusion over this identification of bay, scholars have been reluctant to exclude such a noble plant from the honour of a mention in the Bible—and bay does in fact grow profusely in Carmel, Tabor and Gilead. Possibly in this case bay refers not so much to a specific tree, but simply to a native or indigenous one growing in its natural and sympathetic environment and therefore flourishing and spreading itself luxuriantly. In the right conditions and in a warm climate the bay can grow as tall as 60 feet. In more temperate climates it is usually cultivated as an ornamental shrub, often in a wooden tub, trained as a standard on a central stem with a clipped, rounded top. Bay is evergreen and the leaves have an important place in cookery, and in medicine, which also makes use of the berries.

The bay is associated with victory, success and glory. Victorious athletes and heroes of early Greek and Roman times were crowned with wreaths of bay, and poets were similarly honoured (hence our expression Poet Laureate). According to legend, the tree came into being when the nymph Daphne begged the gods to transform her and destroy her beauty to save her from Apollo's amorous pursuits. So she was turned into a laurel; but even as a tree Apollo loved her, and she shrank from his kisses (Ovid, METAMORPHOSES, Book I).

Students who have taken their degrees at universities are called Bachelor, from the French *bachelier*, which derives from the Latin *baccalaureus* (laurel and berries) and these students were not allowed to marry in case the duties of husband and father should keep them from their literary studies. Thus all single men came to be called bachelors. In France too, the school leaving certificate (giving access to the universities) is called the *baccalauréat*.

Some people chew a bay leaf before meals to aid digestion, by making them salivate, and you can also drink an infusion of the dried leaves for dyspepsia and flatulence. Gerard recommends the juice of the berries as a remedy for 'paine of the eares, and deafenesse' whilst Culpeper claims astonishing powers for them:

> *Seven of them given to a woman in sore travail of child-birth do cause a speedy delivery, and expel the afterbirth . . .*

(*CULPEPER'S* HERBAL)

I'm glad I didn't have to depend on bay berries in these circumstances, although my faith in the virtues of the leaves is without question. You can use them fresh or dried. I put one or two fresh ones in the bottom of the terrine when I make a pâté and they give a subtly spicy flavour and look good too. Bay leaf is also an excellent flavouring for soups, stews, casseroles and marinades, and it is one of the traditional ingredients of the *bouquet garni* (the others are marjoram, thyme and parsley). You can also use bay as a flavouring for milk puddings, as the Victorians did (they used to put the dried leaves in jars of sugar to flavour it), in béchamel sauce, or even in cakes, as in this old family recipe:

BRIDE'S CAKE

375 g ($\frac{3}{4}$ lb) flour

250 g ($\frac{1}{2}$ lb) butter

250 g ($\frac{1}{2}$ lb) caster sugar

4 eggs

750 g ($1\frac{1}{2}$ lb) currants

125 g (4 oz) mixed peel

1 tsp baking powder

2 tbsp treacle

a little milk

2 bay leaves

Cream butter and sugar. Add eggs, beating well. Add flour, currants and peel. Warm milk with bay leaves. Mix with treacle and add baking powder. Bake for approximately 2 hours in a moderate oven.

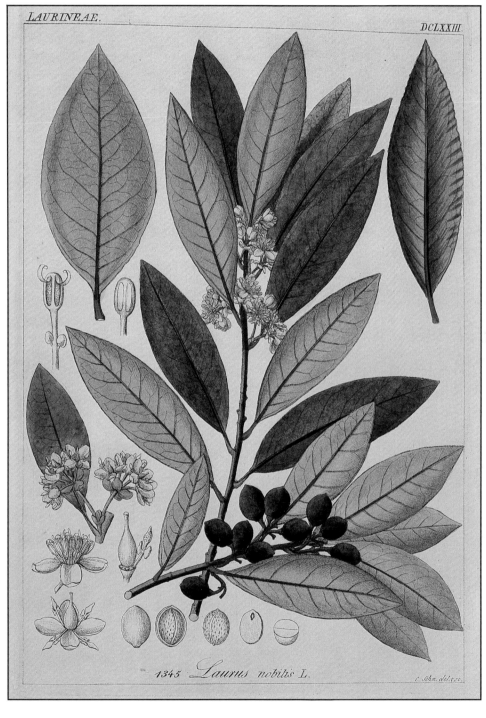

LAURINEAE.

DCLXXIII.

1345 *Laurus nobilis L.*

(LAUREL FAMILY—*LAURACEAE*)

BEAN
Vicia faba

And it came to pass, when David was come to Mahanaim, that Shobi the son of Nahash of Rabbah of the children of Ammon . . . brought beds, and basons, and earthen vessels, and wheat, and barley, and flour, and parched corn, and beans, and lentiles, and parched pulse, and honey, and butter, and sheep, and cheese of kine, for David, and for the people that were with him, to eat: for they said, The people is hungry, and weary, and thirsty, in the wilderness.

(2 SAMUEL 17: 27–29)

The beans here would have been broad beans, which were extensively cultivated in Biblical times and were well-known to the Greeks, Romans and the Egyptians. An important article of diet, they were versatile and could be made into purées and pottages or a coarse type of bread (sometimes mixed with millet). They had the advantage too, with the other pulses, that they could be dried and kept throughout the year, and though cheap they were relished by rich and poor alike. Broad beans have been grown in Britain for centuries, having been introduced by the Romans, and appear frequently in the earliest ever cook-books. They have a homely quality which is irresistible and they even feature in the somewhat pretentious *nouvelle cuisine*—briefly boiled, then sautéed in butter as an accompaniment to roast saddle of lamb. This 19th-century suggestion comes from ELIZA ACTON'S MODERN COOKERY FOR PRIVATE FAMILIES, 1845.

BROAD OR WINDSOR BEANS

When young, freshly gathered and well dressed, these beans, even with many persons accustomed to a luxurious table, are a favourite accompaniment to a dish of streaked bacon or delicate pickled pork. . . . A boiled cheek of bacon, trimmed free of any blackish parts may be dished over the beans on occasion . . . this vegetable is often skinned after it is boiled and then gently tossed up with a little butter before it is dished.

Culpeper warns of the hazard broad beans share with the other pulses: 'Beans eaten are extreme windy meat . . . '!

They are however a good source of protein—vitamin C, iron and dietary fibre too—and are easily grown. In France, summer savory is often planted between the rows and this pretty little herb, which is a favourite of bees, is the classic accompaniment there. You can eat broad beans raw when young, with other vegetables as part of a selection of crudités, or cook them in lightly salted water and serve with a knob of butter, some parsley sauce or chopped chervil. They are good cold too, with vinaigrette, and you can make a delicious pale green purée by putting them through a vegetable mill (which holds back the tough outer skin) and adding salt, black pepper and a little cream.

(PEA FAMILY—*LEGUMINOSAE*)

Vicia Faba L.

BOX   # CYPRESS

Buxus longifolia   *Cupressus sempervirens*

*The glory of Lebanon shall come unto thee, the fir tree, the pine tree, and the
box together, to beautify the place of my sanctuary; and I will make the place
of my feet glorious.*

(ISAIAH 60: 13)

Box in its familiar state is a mere shrub, and it is popularly clipped in the topiary
gardening which the Romans probably initiated. It can become a small tree, however,
if left to grow naturally, though not a particularly attractive one. *Buxus longifolia* is now
restricted to southernmost Turkey, but may have grown further south in biblical times.
It is considered to be the same species taxonomically as the western Mediterranean species
Buxus balearica which is found in Sardinia, southern Spain and the Balearic Isles. However
it is now generally accepted that box in ISAIAH 60 is a mistranslation and that Cypress is
intended. This is much more appropriate to the context—Cypress being a tall and stately
tree.

Cypress has for hundreds of years been associated with death and is a characteristic
feature of old cemeteries:

Come away, come away, death,
And in sad cypress let me be laid;
Fly away, fly away, breath,
I am slain by a fair cruel maid.

My shroud of white, stuck all with yew,
O, prepare it;
My part of death no one so true
Did share it.

Not a flower, not a flower sweet,
on my black coffin let there be strown;
Not a friend, not a friend greet
My poor corps, where my bones shall be thrown.

A thousand thousand sighs to save,
Lay me, O, where,
Sad true lover never find my grave,
To weep there.

(*Shakespeare:* TWELFTH NIGHT, *Act II, scene 4*)

This emblem of grief owes its name to the beautiful youth Cyparissus who was dearly
loved by Apollo, and who accidentally killed a favourite and wonderfully tame stag sacred
to the nymphs of Carthaea. The boy could not be cured of his grief and begged as a last
gift from the gods that he might be allowed to grieve forever. And so he was changed
into a cypress tree.

The wood has an incorruptible quality—it is fragrant, compact and hard and was used by the Egyptians for making sarcophagi and by the Greeks for statues of their gods:

Theophrastus attributeth great honor to this tree, shewing that the roofes of old temples became famous by reason of that wood, and that the timber thereof, of which the rafters are made, is everlasting, and is not hurt there by rotting, cobweb, nor any infirmitie or corruption.

(Gerard's HERBALL, 1597)

Cypress is still put to medicinal use, internally as an astringent, or externally a decoction of the cones is applied in hot compresses for the treatment of painful piles. It is supposed to be good for sweaty feet too, as a footbath—soak your feet for ten or fifteen minutes.

1140. Cupressus sempervirens L.

(BOX FAMILY—*BUXACEAE*)

(CYPRESS FAMILY—*CUPRESSACEAE*)

BRAMBLE
Rubus sanguineus

For a good tree bringeth not forth corrupt fruit; neither doth a corrupt tree bring forth good fruit. For every tree is known by his own fruit. For of thorns men do not gather figs, nor of a bramble bush gather they grapes.

(LUKE 6: 43–44)

About twenty Hebrew words are used in the Bible to express prickly shrubs or weeds which are variously translated as *bramble, brier, thorn, thistle* ... but the above quotation clearly refers to the true bramble, *Rubus sanguineus*, which is common in thorny thickets in central and northern Israel. In Jotham's parable, the bramble is chosen as King of the trees, after the vine and olive have refused the honour:

And the bramble said unto the trees, If in truth ye anoint me king over you, then come and put your trust in my shadow: and if not, let fire come out of the bramble, *and devour the cedars of Lebanon.*

(JUDGES 9: 15)

One of the most common and familiar plants in temperate countries, there are about 250 species, plus innumerable self-reproducing variants of these species. The bramble is unusual in so far as on a single branch can be found both flowers and fruits at various stages of ripeness. Bramble plants are very prickly, but the fresh leaves crushed between the fingers and rubbed on the skin will stop the bleeding which the thorns have inflicted, an interesting example of nature's harmony.

All parts of the plant have been used medicinally for hundreds of years:

The leaves and brambles, as well green as dry, are excellent good lotions for sores in the mouth or secret parts

says Culpeper, and recent research shows that blackberry juice has an extraordinary vitalising property. You can make a decoction of the dried leaves by boiling one to two ounces in a quart of water, and this is good for inflammations of the mouth and throat. But the jam, jelly or syrup, apart from being delicious, is also an excellent treatment for sore throats, diarrhoea and enteritis—the fruit having 'a certaine kinde of astriction or binding qualitie.' (Gerard)

There are hundreds of excellent recipes for brambles and the simple country wine made from them is one of the best, with a strong suggestion of the wonderful wines of Rioja. Here's one of my favourite pudding recipes:

AUTUMN PUDDING

750 g (1½ lb) brambles
8 thin slices of day-old bread
2 tbsp water
100 g (4 oz) caster sugar or to taste

Remove the crusts from the bread and use the slices to line a pudding basin, making sure that there are no gaps. Keep enough for the top. Pick over the brambles and put in a saucepan with 2 tbsp water and sugar to taste. Cook until the sugar is dissolved and the juice begins to flow. Save some of the juice. Turn the fruit into the lined basin and cover with a lid of bread. Put a plate on top that fits exactly inside the dish, and weight it. Leave overnight in a cool place. Turn it out and pour over any surplus juice. Serve with cream.[5]

It is supposed to be unlucky to eat brambles after Michaelmas Day (29 September) since the devil is supposed to urinate on them after that date. However, in northern countries they seldom ripen before then.

RUBUS, RONCE. N°. 1.   Page 234 *

(ROSE FAMILY—*ROSACEAE*)

BULRUSH

Cyperus papyrus

And the woman conceived, and bare a son: and when she saw him that he was a goodly child, she hid him three months. And when she could not longer hide him, she took for him an ark of bulrushes, *and daubed it with slime and with pitch, and put the child therein; and she laid it in the flags by the river's brink.*

(EXODUS 2: 2–3)

The story of the baby Moses in his basket of bulrushes is one of the most romantic and evocative of the Old Testament, absorbed by children in infant classes and always remembered. But the plant of which Moses' basket was made was in fact *papyrus*, a sub-tropical plant of the vast sedge family which had various economic uses—mainly fuel, baskets and sailing vessels of various sorts:

Woe to the land shadowing with wings, which is beyond the rivers of Ethiopia:
That sendeth ambassadors by the sea, even in vessels of bulrushes *upon the waters . . .*

(ISAIAH 18: 1–2)

And it was the buoyant stalks of this plant which the famous Thor Heyerdahl used to construct his transatlantic vessels *Ra I* and *Ra II*.

Of course, its most famous use is as the writing material which was made from the pith. Gerard calls it paper reed:

This kinde of reede which I have englished Paper reede, or Paper plant, is the same, (as I do reade,) that paper was made of in Egypt, before the invention of paper made of linnen clouts, was found out . . . the same reede mentioned in the second chapter of EXODUS: *whereof was made that basket or cradle. . . .*

The Greeks called the pith of papyrus *byblos*, and the books of papyrus sheets *bybla* and it is from this that our word *Bible* is derived.

The paper was made by laying strips of the pith side by side, then placing another layer at right angles and pressing and drying it to form a sheet. Rush or reed pens were used to write with.

And when I looked, behold, an hand was sent unto me; and, lo, a roll of a book was therein; and he spread it before me; and it was written within and without: and there was written therein lamentations, and mourning, and woe.

(EZEKIEL 2: 9–10)

(SEDGE FAMILY—CYPERACEAE)

CALAMUS SWEET CANE

Cymbopogon martinii   *Acorus calamus*

> *Take thou also unto thee principal spices, of pure myrrh five hundred shekels,
> and of sweet cinnamon half so much, even two hundred and fifty shekels,
> and of* sweet calamus *two hundred and fifty shekels, And of cassia five
> hundred shekels, after the shekel of the sanctuary, and of oil olive an hin:
> And thou shalt make it an oil of holy ointment, an ointment compound after
> the art of the apothecary: it shall be an holy anointing oil.*
>
> (EXODUS 30: 23–25)

Scented grasses and aromatic plants were important in Biblical times for medicinal and
flavouring purposes as well as for cosmetics, perfumes and oils such as the one above,
for which the children of Israel were given directions as Moses led them across the desert
to the promised land.

Ginger grass or sweet calamus (*Cymbopogon martinii*) was probably one of these: others
are *Cymbopogon citratus* (lemon grass) and *Cymbopogon schoenanthus* (camel grass). Some
of these grasses were found during the 19th-century excavations of the tombs of the
Pharaohs—amazingly still retaining their perfume—and while some may have been
indigenous, most were imported:

> *To what purpose cometh there to me incense from Sheba, and the* sweet cane
> *from a far country? your burnt offerings are not acceptable, nor your
> sacrifices sweet unto me.*
>
> (JEREMIAH 6: 20)

Sweet sedge, sweetflag and sweet cane are all names for *Acorus calamus*. The leaves
resemble those of the beautiful yellow flag (*Iris pseudacorus*) though in fact it is not an
iris, but a member of the Arum family, and all parts of the plant are fragrant. Because of
this it was greatly used as a strewing herb and even recently was used as such in Norwich
Cathedral for important festivals. Cardinal Wolsey also enjoyed having his floors strewn
with calamus and this was one of the charges of extravagance against him—it didn't grow
near London, so had to be fetched at great cost from other parts of the country.

Although it is a native of India, sweetflag is now naturalised in Europe and is found
growing locally throughout England. An emergent aquatic, it grows in water close to the
margins of rivers, streams or ditches and is associated with reeds and bulrushes.

The dried rhizome has been used medicinally for centuries.

> *It is of great effect, being put in broth or taken in fumes through a close
> stoole, to provoke womens naturall accidents.*
>
> (*Gerard's* HERBALL *1597*)

But more recently calamus has been used as an aromatic, stimulant tonic or for
dyspepsia. It has a spicy flavour and Culpeper recommends it, 'put into sauce for fish'.

It has also been used as an ingredient of snuff, for hair and tooth powders, and the oil
which it contains is used in perfumery.

You can buy it in good herbalists, and there are many interesting old pot-pourri, sweet
bag and pomander recipes to try. This one is from Mary Dogget's BOOK OF RECIPES, 1682.

RECEIPT FOR A SWEET BAGG

Take half a pound of Cypress Roots, a pound of Orris, $\frac{3}{4}$ lb Rhodium, a pound coriander seed, $\frac{3}{4}$ lb of calamus, 3 oranges stuck with cloves, 2 ounces of Benjamin, and an ounce of storax and 4 pecks of Damask Rose leaves, a peck of dried sweet marjerum, a pretty stick of Juniper shaved very thin, some lemon peel dryed; let all these be powdered very grosely for the first year and immediately put into your baggs; the next year pound and work it and it will be very good again.

SMILACEAE: *Acorinae.*   CCCCXXIX.

956 Acorus Calamus L.

(GRASS FAMILY—*GRAMINEAE*) (ARUM FAMILY—*ARACEAE*)

CAMPHIRE

(Henna) *Lawsonia inermis*

My beloved is unto me as a cluster of camphire *in the vineyards of Engedi.*

(SONG OF SOLOMON 1: 14)

Henna, or camphire as it was then known, is only mentioned twice in the Bible, in the SONG OF SOLOMON—in erotic context:

> *A garden inclosed is my sister, my spouse; a spring shut up, a fountain sealed. Thy plants are an orchard of pomegranates, with pleasant fruits; camphire, with spikenard.*

(SONG OF SOLOMON 4: 12–13)

A member of the loosestrife family, henna is a tropical and sub-tropical tree-like shrub which is covered with long lilac-like clusters of delicate yellowish/white flowers in the spring. Camphire has always been popular for its fragrance, though some westerners find the odour somewhat stifling. It smells much like roses; an essential oil, 'mehendi' is distilled from the flowers and used as perfume and in religious feasts. Camphire was also used by women to decorate their apartments, to wear in their hair and their bosoms, and it was believed that bunches of the flowers hanging from the ceiling would purify the air.

Henna is a household word to us, mainly as a shampoo-dye (for hair). This was its most important use in Biblical times too, not so much for hair, but for the nails and skin.

> *The females of the higher and middle classes, and many of the poorer women, stain certain parts of their hands and feet (which are, with very few exceptions, beautifully formed,) with the leaves of the henna-tree, which impart a yellowish red or deep orange colour. Many thus dye only the nails of the fingers and toes; others extend the dye as high as the first joint of each finger and toe; some also make a stripe along the next row of joints; and there are several other fanciful modes of applying the henna. . . . The colour does not disappear until after many days: it is generally renewed after about a fortnight or three weeks. To the nails, the henna imparts a more bright, clear and permanent colour than to the skin.*
>
> (AN ACCOUNT OF THE MANNERS AND CUSTOMS OF THE MODERN EGYPTIANS
> LANE, 1860)

The Egyptians also used henna for dyeing the clothes in which their mummies were wrapped.

Muslim brides were even more elaborately decorated—using strips of cotton which were wrapped around their limbs to resist the dye. Old women used to dye their hair too with henna, and different shades could be obtained by mixing with the leaves of other plants such as indigo.

Medicinally, the bark was used by the Arabs, and the leaves and flowers for the treatment of jaundice, smallpox and skin disorders.

(LOOSESTRIFE FAMILY—*LYTHRACEAE*)

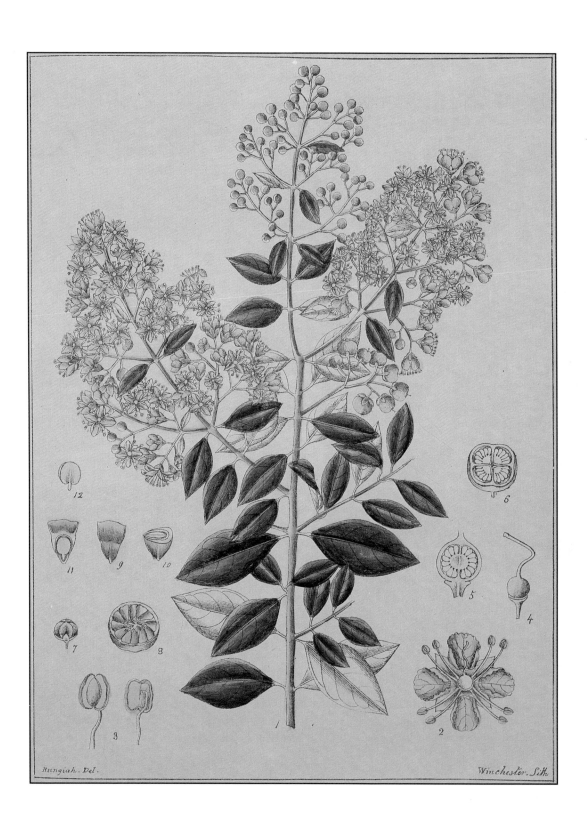

CAROB

Ceratonia siliqua

And he would fain have filled his belly with the husks that the swine did eat: and no man gave unto him. And when he came to himself, he said, How many hired servants of my father's have bread enough and to spare, and I perish with hunger!

(LUKE 15: 16–17)

This was the prodigal son of the parable. He had 'wasted his substance with riotous living', was now reduced to extreme hunger and longed for those 'husks' which were generally fodder for cattle and swine.

Sometimes translated 'pods', it is almost certain that the fruit of the carob tree is what is meant, and it is more than likely that *locusts* in MATTHEW 3: 4 refers to this also—rather than to the grasshopper-like insect whose visitations were frequently a sign of divine displeasure. (Locusts were one of the plagues sent for the punishment of the Egyptians.)

And the same John had his raiment of camel's hair, and a leathern girdle about his loins; and his meat was locusts *and wild honey.*

(MATTHEW 3: 4)

Not that locusts (the insects) were not relished in the Middle East. This was the traveller Jackson writing of life in 19th century Morocco:

Locusts are esteemed a great delicacy . . . there are various ways of dressing them; that usually adopted is to boil them in water half an hour, then sprinkle them with salt and pepper, and fry them, adding a little vinegar. The head, wings, and legs are thrown away, the rest of the body is eaten, and resembles the taste of prawns . . . A person may eat a plate full of them, containing two or three hundred, without any ill effects.[6]

The carob tree (also called 'St John's bread' in many languages) is an important native tree in Israel, which oddly enough isn't mentioned at all in the *Old Testament*, nor even specifically in the *New*. It is common on Mediterranean coasts and the sweet, chocolate-flavoured ripe pods are popular with Italian children—you can buy them at most country markets there. The pods are about the size of a banana, but flat and very dark brown. When completely ripe they are full of a sweet dark-coloured syrup as well as the seeds. Because it does not contain caffeine, carob powder has become a fashionable substitute for cocoa, and vegetarian and 'health' cook-books have many recipes for carob cakes, sweets, biscuits and sauces. If using carob powder instead of cocoa, use only half as much and expect very dark brown results. Gerard refers to carob briefly in his HERBALL:

These cods being dry are very like bean cods; as I have often seen. I have sowen the seeds in my garde, where they have prospered exceeding wel.

The seeds are remarkably uniform in size and they are said to have been the original 'carat' weight used in the measuring of precious stones, mostly diamonds.

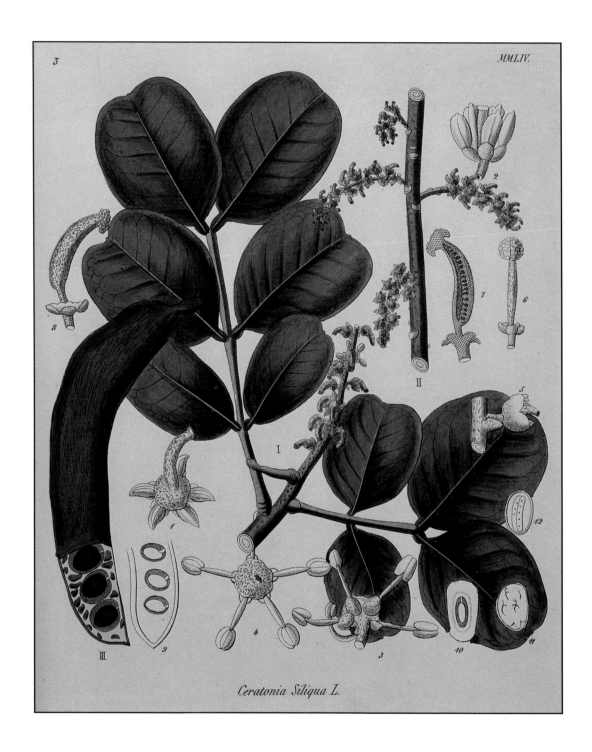

Ceratonia Siliqua L.

(PEA FAMILY—*LEGUMINOSAE*)

CASSIA CINNAMON

Cinnamomum aromaticum   *Cinnamomum verum*

Thou lovest righteousness, and hatest wickedness: therefore God, thy God, hath anointed thee with the oil of gladness above thy fellows. All thy garments smell of myrrh, and aloes, and cassia, *out of the ivory palaces, whereby they have made thee glad.*

(PSALMS 45: 7–8)

Both expensive and exotic imports in biblical times, cassia and cinnamon are broadly similar—cassia is sometimes called *bastard cinnamon*, implying its use as a substitute for *Cinnamomum verum*. They are sometimes found together, as ingredients of the holy anointing oil, for example, which Moses is instructed to make with myrrh, sweet cinnamon, sweet calamus, cassia and olive oil (EXODUS 30: 23–24). Spices and perfumes were by no means confined to the religious context of holy oils and incenses or for purification or embalming—their sensual and aphrodisiac qualities were always greatly prized.

I have perfumed my bed with myrrh, aloes, and cinnamon. *Come, let us take our fill of love until the morning: let us solace ourselves with loves.*

(PROVERBS 7: 17–18)

The bark of both plants is used but that of cassia is somewhat coarser and darker, and has a less delicate flavour. Its immature fruits resemble cloves and they were used in *hippocras*, the spiced wine of medieval times or in pot-pourri. Cassia is a native of eastern Asia, so was a somewhat precious commodity in the Middle East and its oil was used both for anointing and for incense. Medicinally it was known to be a powerful germicide and has been used to decrease the secretion of milk, though it has been used more generally to assist and flavour other drugs.

Ceylon cinnamon is scarcer and therefore more expensive. It grows in almost pure sand, and has antiseptic, astringent and stimulant properties. Commercial cinnamon bark is the dried inner bark of the shoots, and is sweet, fragrant and aromatic. As a flavouring it has been prized for hundreds of years: the Romans imported cinnamon, cassia and other spices to England to enliven their cuisine and in the medieval period cinnamon was extensively used with cloves and mace in pies and tarts, in breads, meat stews, and in fish dishes.

Sometimes the ground cinnamon was pounded with other spices to make a powder for sprinkling on roasted apples, quinces and pears:

BLANCH POWDER
50 g (2 oz) sugar
6 g ($\frac{1}{4}$ oz) ginger
3 g ($\frac{1}{8}$ oz) cinnamon
beaten small to a powder
(*Thomas Cogan,* THE HAVEN OF HEALTH, *1596*)

Gerard mentions both *cinnamon* and *cassia of Dioscorides and the Antients* and recommends the latter used in larger quantity for the same purpose as cinnamon:

Out of the berries of this tree is drawne by expression, as out of the berries of the Olive tree, a certain oyle, or rather a kinde of fat like butter, without any smell at all, except it be made warme, and then it smelleth as the cinnamon doth, and is much used against the coldnes of the sinewes, all paines of the joints. . . .

Cinnamon is still used extensively in cookery, in cakes, buns, breads and curry powders. Often the best flavour is obtained by adding a piece of the bark to the dish rather than using the ground spice, for example in cooking moussaka. Cinnamon, ground or crushed, has also been a popular spice to add to pot-pourri, sweet jars, or sachets to scent linen and notepaper.

Laurus Cinnamonum.

(LAUREL FAMILY—*LAURACEAE*)

CEDAR OF LEBANON
Cedrus libani

Behold, the Assyrian was a cedar in Lebanon with fair branches, and with a shadowing shroud, and of an high stature; and his top was among the thick boughs. . . .

(EZEKIEL 31: 3)

Handsome, elegant, dignified, the cedar of Lebanon symbolises strength and nobility in the Bible, and was considered sovereign of trees. It is an evergreen emanating from the high, snow-clad mountains of Lebanon, and thrives on poor stony soil. It has a distinctive appearance with thick overspreading horizontal branches which, according to Evelyn's SILVA, 'when agitated by the wind, play in the most graceful manner. . . .'

The trees of the LORD are full of sap; the cedars of Lebanon, which he hath planted; Where the birds make their nests. . . .

(PSALMS 104: 16–17)

Cedars are still called 'trees of the Lord' by Arabs, and they are mighty indeed, growing as high as 120 feet and of enormous girth—they rival the olive for longevity, sometimes reaching an age of more than 2,000 years. Muslims revere trees generally but the enjoyment of the shade of an old cedar is a particular luxury and many prefer to pray there rather than in the mosque.

Gerard includes cedar of Lebanon in his HERBALL of 1597, but doesn't mention ever seeing it in England. Two were certainly planted in the physic garden of Chelsea around 1683 and Archibald, Duke of Argyll, planted some at Whitton. John Evelyn obtained seeds and cones from the few trees remaining at Libanus and strongly recommended planting them:

. . . why they should not thrive in old England, I know not, save for want of industry and trial.

They are now naturalised in many parts of the country and might even be more common here than in their ancient birthplace. Travellers over the centuries have certainly commented on the scarcity of cedars on the mountains which produced timber so valuable that Solomon exchanged cities with Hiram for it. Solomon planted cedars in Judea however, and from then it became a Jewish custom to plant a cedar when a son was born, and a pine for a girl. At the time of the child's marriage the tree would be cut down to form the nuptial bed. Cedar was a symbol of purity and constancy because of its incorruptible nature.

The Egyptians imported it from earliest times for use in ship-building, for houses, carvings and for coffins. The pitch was also used in the embalming process.

Solomon's temple was largely constructed of cedar, and some idea of the extent of the forest and its subsequent devastation may be guessed from 1 KINGS 5: 15:

And Solomon had threescore and ten thousand that bare burdens, and fourscore thousand hewers in the mountains. . . .

The logs were floated down from the coast of Lebanon on large rafts.

Apart from being extremely durable, the wood is fragrant and beautiful, and its bitterness keeps it free of worm. The rosin had its medicinal uses too:

It was also recommended for leprosy, worms, nits, lice and for toothache! Cedar wood is still prized for the same reasons as in biblical times, and the shavings or the oil, which you can buy in herbalists, make a fragrant addition to pot pourri or sweet bags.

(PINE FAMILY—*PINACEAE*)

CHESTNUT TREE

(Oriental Plane) *Platanus orientalis*

And Jacob took him rods of green poplar, and of the hazel and chestnut tree; and pilled white strakes in them, and made the white appear which was in the rods. And he set the rods which he had pilled before the flocks in the gutters in the watering troughs when the flocks came to drink, that they should conceive when they came to drink. And the flocks conceived before the rods, and brought forth cattle ringstraked, speckled, and spotted.

(GENESIS 30: 37–39)

Jacob peeled the bark off the poplar, almond and chestnut so that the streaked twigs would increase the number of pied animals in the herd. But chestnut (*Castanea sativa*) is not indigenous to Syria or Palestine and has probably never grown there except as an exotic. The plane tree, *Platanus orientalis*, however, grows everywhere by watercourses and is one of the finest trees in the country—second in stature and dignity only to the cedar of Lebanon, and it is generally accepted that this is the tree referred to above, and in EZEKIEL 31: 8 (its bark peels off easily exposing a naked white trunk.)

The Greeks and Romans revered the tree for its shade and Pliny (quoted by Gerard, 1597) reports that they were 'woont to be cherished with wine ... it is founde by experience that the same is very comfortable to the rootes ... trees desire to drink wine'!

Plane trees were introduced into England about the middle of the 16th century. Turner reports in 1551:

> *I have sene ... two very yong trees in England, which were called there Playn trees.*

Although late to produce its leaves and shedding them early, it gives a delightful shade in summer:

> *The Turks in Constantinople seem to enjoy no greater luxury than that of reclining under the umbrageous boughs of these majestic trees, and smoking their tobacco in a state of perfect indifference to all sublunary things,*

writes Henry Phillips in Sylva Florifera of 1823, and it's an interesting fact too, that this tree is never injured by insect or blight, and protects itself from moss and other parasites by shedding its bark annually. The plane tree has always thrived in smoky urban areas and was thought to be a purifier of the air and even a defence against plague. In the 18th century lime trees became more popular for walks and avenues because they were easier to propogate and grew more quickly in the first few years, but the plane is not difficult to cultivate. It is generally raised from layers, but you can obtain better specimens by sowing ripe seed in a moist situation, or by planting cuttings early in autumn in moist good soil. If you water them frequently, you will ensure as rapid a growth as watering with wine did in ancient times.

Although late to produce its leaves and shedding them early, it gives a delightful shade in summer and the leaves are never attacked by insects or blight. It was thought that the plane tree was a purifier of the air and even a defence against plague. In the 18th century lime trees became more popular for avenues because they were easier to propagate and grew more quickly in the first few years, but the plane is not difficult to cultivate. It is generally raised from layers, but you can obtain better specimens by sowing ripe seed in a moist situation, or by planting cuttings early in autumn in moist, good soil. If you water them frequently, you will ensure as rapid a growth as watering with wine did in ancient times!

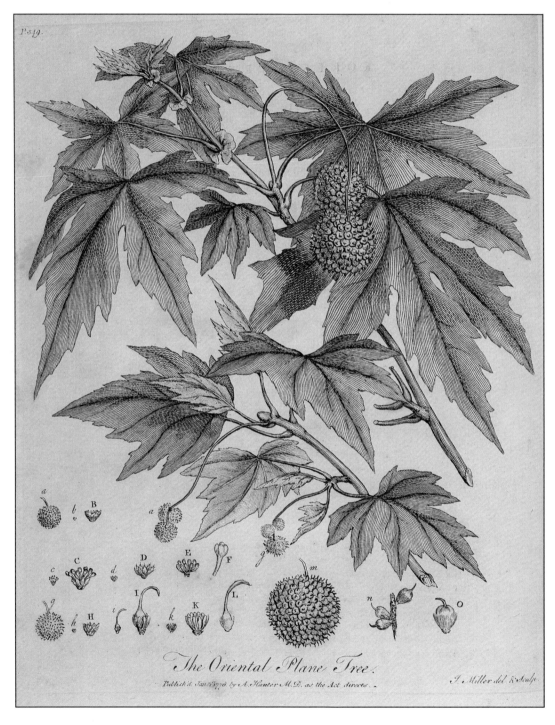

The Oriental Plane Tree.

Publish'd Jan.ry 1776 by A. Hunter M.D. as the Act directs.

J. Miller del. & Sculp.

(PLANE-TREE FAMILY—*PLATANACEAE*)

CORIANDER

Coriandrum sativum

Coriander is only referred to twice in the Bible in comparison to the miraculous food manna which was sent to the Israelites in the desert:

> *And the house of Israel called the name thereof* Manna: *and it was like* coriander *seed, white; and the taste of it was like wafers made with honey.*
>
> (EXODUS 16: 31)

There have been many attempts to explain the heavenly food manna, which God provided daily for the Israelites for forty years, but it remains persistently on the supernatural level. One suggestion of the late 19th century was that manna was a sweet substance exuded by insects feeding on the tamarisk tree. This is certainly collected by the Bedouin and used as a substitute for honey, but in such small quantities (and only seasonally) that it could have provided no more than a passing treat for anyone wandering in the desert—tamarisks being relatively scarce.

There is no confusion about coriander however. It is a member of the carrot family and is a native of Israel, though was once widely cultivated. Coriander is still used extensively in cookery and also has some medicinal value both as an aromatic, carminative tonic, and to disguise the taste of purgatives and other disagreeable medicines.

When fresh, the plant smells rather unpleasant but the odour improves on drying. The seeds are an important aromatic ingredient of curry powders and they have been popular over the centuries in traditional breads and cakes—often for medicinal reasons:

> *Coriandre layd to wyth breade or barly mele is good for Saynt Antonyes Fyre.*
>
> (*Turner's* HERBAL, *1551*)

(St Anthony's Fire being the name given to erysipelas, because it was believed that St Anthony could cure it.)

Coriander was cultivated by the Romans in Britain but its use as a flavouring goes back to the Bronze Age and seeds were found by archaeologists in a late Bronze Age hut at Minnis Bay, Kent, the earliest example of an imported spice from the Mediterranean.

> *Coriander seede prepared and covered with sugar, as comfits, taken after meate closeth up the mouthe of the stomacke, staieth vomiting, and helpeth digestion.*

writes Gerard and the seeds were also added to liqueurs for the same purpose.

You can grow coriander easily in your garden. Plant the seeds in spring in a well-drained sunny place. Plants grow to about 75 cm (2½ feet) and the seeds ripen around August. Leave the seed heads in a warm place to dry, before stripping them and storing the seeds in air-tight containers. Their aroma and flavour develop with age.

SWEET SCENTED BAGS TO LAY WITH LINEN

Eight ounces of damask rose leaves, eight ounces of coriander seeds, eight ounces of sweet orris root, eight ounces of calamus aromaticus, one ounce of mace, one ounce of cinnamon, half an ounce of cloves, four drachms of musk-powder, two drachms of white loaf sugar, three ounces of lavender flowers and some of rhodium wood. Beat them well together and make them in small silk bags.

(*Hannah Glasse,* THE ART OF COOKERY, *1784*)

RATATOUILLE NIÇOISE

This classic Provençal vegetable stew has a flavouring of coriander seeds.

2 aubergines
2 large onions
2 red or green peppers
500 g (1 1b) courgettes
1 tsp coriander seeds
3-4 tomatoes
olive oil
2-3 cloves garlic
salt, pepper
parsley

Vary the vegetables according to availability. Wash the aubergines and cut them into cubes. Put them in a colander, sprinkle with salt and leave them for an hour. Chop the onions and cut the peppers into thin strips. Cut the courgettes into rounds, and skin and chop the tomatoes. Cook the onions gently in olive oil, and when they are softening, add the peppers and the aubergines, dried in a napkin. Cook gently for a few minutes, then add the courgettes. Crush the garlic and add it with the skinned tomatoes and crushed coriander. Cover the pan and cook slowly until the vegetables are tender but not mushy. Season, sprinkle with chopped parsley and serve with garlic bread.[7]

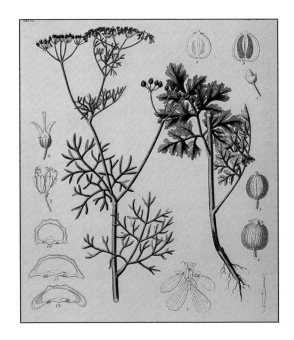

(CARROT FAMILY—*UMBELLIFERAE*)

CUCUMBER MUSK MELON

Cucumis sativus   *Cucumis melo*

> *We remember the fish, which we did eat in Egypt freely; the* cucumbers, *and the* melons, *and the* leeks, *and the* onions, *and the* garlick. . . .
>
> (NUMBERS 11: 5)

The Israelites are complaining here of their unvaried diet of manna in the wilderness. *'There is nothing at all, beside this manna, before our eyes.'* (NUMBERS 11: 6)

Scholars mostly agree that garden cucumbers (*Cucumis sativus*) were unlikely to have been cultivated in Bible lands at that period. The Israelites were almost certainly longing for musk melons (*Cucumis melo*), the fruits of a tropical plant which originated in East Africa and has some similarity to the cucumber. It was, and still is, widely cultivated in Egypt and is considered to be the finest of all the cucumber and melon-like fruits, being called by one author, 'The Queen of the Cucumbers'.

As valuable an article of diet as cucumbers, fields of these melons were closely guarded against theft, and look-out 'lodges' made of twigs and matting such as the one mentioned below are still used today.

> *And the daughter of Zion is left as a cottage in a vineyard, as a lodge in a garden of* cucumbers, *as a besieged city.*
>
> (ISAIAH 1: 8)

To readers of the 17th-century Bible, cucumbers were certainly familiar fruit and Gerard mentions several varieties as well as muske-melons and gourds—with directions for cultivation. Some were small, like gherkins, others pear-shaped and some were persuaded to grow artificially, by encasing the embryonic fruit in a hollow cane. The Victorians liked colourful cucumbers—white, yellow, bronze and bluish, as well as the normal green ones and they had names such as 'Lord Roberts', 'The Long Gun' and 'Doctor Livingstone'.

Medicinally they were valued for their cooling and cleansing properties rather than for their nourishment (they contain 96 per cent water) and were used externally for the treatment of sunburn, inflammations, sore eyes, spots, pimples, and to 'make the skin smooth and faire'. Taking them internally in a potage of mutton, oatmeal and herbs was supposed to have a similar effect.

Cucumbers are available all the year round, and foreign travel has expanded an enjoyment of their possibilities. Chilled gazpacho from Spain, Scandinavian pickles, yoghurt and cucumber soups and salads from the Middle East, *concombres à la crème* from France, mousses, dips and of course in wafer-thin slices for those most English of dainty tea-time sandwiches. (For these it's best to salt the cucumber lightly for half an hour or so between two plates then to squeeze out the water).

You can buy cooling cucumber hand creams, face lotions, soaps and bubble baths, or you can make your own. Here is a simple face lotion which is good for sunburn: Chop up a cucumber, squeeze out the juice and mix with equal quantities of glycerine and rose water.

And you can make a delicious version of the chilled soup, *vichyssoise*, using unpeeled cucumbers instead of leeks—or this simple cucumber and yoghurt soup, which is uncooked:

CUCUMBER AND YOGHURT SOUP
2 cucumbers peeled, seeded and chopped
750 ml (1¼ pt) Yoghurt
½ onion, chopped, or
3-4 spring onions
salt
garnish
cucumber—thin slices
1 tbsp dill if available

Blend the cucumber with the onion and yoghurt in a blender or food processor until just smooth. Add salt to taste and chill before serving with a garnish of cucumber slices and chopped dill.

(PUMPKIN FAMILY—CUCURBITACEAE)

CUMMIN

Cuminum cyminum

Woe unto you, scribes and Pharisees, hypocrites! for ye pay tithe of mint and anise and cummin, and have omitted the weightier matters of the law, judgment, mercy, and faith: these ought ye to have done, and not to leave the other undone.

(MATTHEW 23: 23)

The Jews were not obliged by law to give the tithe of herbs such as these—which could hardly have been considered income, in the way that grain or vegetable crops were. Christ is not criticising the Pharisees for their exactness in doing so, but complaining that while observing such minutiae they neglect the more important issues of justice and truth.

Cummin is a native of the Middle East, but has been cultivated from earliest times for flavouring and medicine. In the 13th century B.C., cummin was used by the Minoans, and Egyptians sprinkled the seed on bread and cakes. It was a popular plant in medieval herb gardens along with other imports such as coriander, fennel and dill which could be persuaded to grow in cooler climates, and, much earlier, it was used by the Celts of the Atlantic coast of France as a flavouring for fish baked with salt and vinegar.

Its popularity as a condiment is now more or less confined to curry powders or other spice mixtures such as garam masala, and it is generally considered inferior in flavour and aroma to the somewhat similar caraway. Medicinally the ground seed was used by the Romans (with wine or bread) and it was also well-known to the Greeks, who associated it with avarice—a miser was said to have eaten cummin! Like dill and fennel it was used as a carminative:

The seedes of Cumin scattereth and breaketh all the windines of the stomacke, belly, guts, and matrix: it is good against the griping torments, gnawing, or fretting of the belly, not onely received inwardly by the mouth, but also in glisters, and outwardly applied to the belly with wine and barly meale boiled togither to the forme of a pultis.

(*Gerard's* HERBALL, *1597*)

Nowadays it is rarely used medicinally, except by vets, as it has a rather bitter taste. Cummin is a member of the *Umbelliferae* or Carrot family, with small white flowers and leaves rather like fennel, though more finely cut. It is no longer common in gardens but it is perfectly possible to grow it for seed as far north as Norway. You should start off the seeds indoors in peat pots, then transfer them to a cold frame before transplanting them to a well-drained, sunny spot. Gather the seed heads when ripe, dry them in a warm place, then strip them from the stems and store in an air-tight jar.

FOR THE RELIEF OF HAEMORRHOIDS
(Italian recipe)

Infusion: 4 g ($\frac{1}{4}$ oz) cummin seeds in a litre (2 pt) of boiling water. Allow to cool then filter and use as a refreshing wash.[9]

(CARROT FAMILY—*UMBELLIFERAE*)

CUMINUM CYMINUM, *Linn.*

DOVE'S DUNG

(Star of Bethlehem) *Ornithogalum umbellatum*

And there was a great famine in Samaria: and, behold, they besieged it, until an ass's head was sold for fourscore pieces of silver, and the fourth part of a cab of dove's dung *for five pieces of silver.*

(2 KINGS 6: 25)

This is the only mention of dove's dung in the Bible, and it has been variously interpreted over the years—as a kind of moss that grows on trees or stony ground, or a variety of pulse or pea, or even literally—as pigeon's dung which can be valuable as a fertilizer for crops, particularly melons. It is now generally agreed however that dove's dung is the rather unromantic name given to that pretty little plant, the Star of Bethlehem, which is related to the onion and garlic.

Named in memory of Christ's nativity and the journey of the Three Kings, the star-like flowers are a brilliant white inside, with petals striped outside with green. The leaves are long, narrow and grassy-looking and when the plants are in blossom the plains and hillsides of Israel look as if they are covered in pigeon-guano (though the name actually comes from the Greek meaning bird's-milk flower). Like many plants of the Lily family, the bulbs are edible and can be eaten raw or roasted like chestnuts. They used to be dried too, and taken on journeys, particularly on pilgrimages to Mecca.

The flowers close early and always close in dull weather, hence local names like 'nap at noon', 'peep o' day', 'eleven o'clock lady' (French *dame d'onze heures*). Star of Bethlehem, for all its charm, is considered a troublesome weed in the USA and is poisonous to cattle in both the fresh state and dried in hay. Gerard mentions six varieties of these 'field onions' in his HERBALL of 1597 but the only one which is truly native to Britain, *Ornithogalum pyrenaicum* is found locally in only a few counties of England. Known as Bath asparagus, the unexpanded flowers used to be gathered in spring and sold in bunches in that town—in the same way that the young shoots of the wild hop are still sold in the north of Italy and served as a seasonal delicacy in omelettes and risottos.

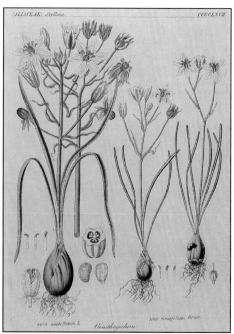

(LILY FAMILY—*LILIACEAE*)

Ornithogalum umbellatum.

ELM

(Terebinth) *Pistacia atlantica, Pistacia palaestina*

. . . for the spirit of whoredoms hath caused them to err, and they have gone a whoring from under their God. They sacrifice upon the tops of the mountains, and burn incense upon the hills, under oaks and poplars and elms, *because the shadow thereof is good: therefore your daughters shall commit whoredom, and your spouses shall commit adultery.*

(HOSEA 4: 12–13)

Elm is only once mentioned in the King James translation of the Bible, and erroneously at that. The Hebrew *elâh* in fact means *terebinth*, and this is the tree which should be understood in many places where *oak* is given. There has been much confusion over the centuries as to the meaning of the several Hebrew words which refer to these two trees, but they were both similarly revered for their longevity and for their sacred associations. Terebinth stands were used for worship, ritual, and as burial places. Abraham entertained three angels under a terebinth (GENESIS 18: 8) and an angel appeared before Gideon under this tree (JUDGES 6: 11). Less felicitous was Absalom's encounter with a terebinth, when he met his end, his hair entangled in its branches:

And Absalom rode upon a mule, and the mule went under the thick boughs of a great oak, *and his head caught hold of the* oak, *and he was taken up between the heaven and the earth; and the mule that was under him went away.*

(2 SAMUEL 18: 9)

The tree is deciduous, with a very thick gnarled trunk, long branches with slender twigs and feathery leaves, minute flowers and fragrant fruit. These used to be taken 'to provoke urine and stir up fleshly lust' (Gerard), and all parts of the tree were used medicinally. It was called the turpentine tree in the early herbals and it exudes a brownish-yellow sticky resin which was greatly valued.

The right Turpentine issueth out of the branches of these trees, if you do cut or wound them, the which is faire and cleere, and better than that which is gathered from the barke of the Firre tree.

(*Gerard's* HERBALL *1597*)

Commercially however, various species of pine are used nowadays for the distillation of oil of turpentine and rosin, and the terebinth of the Middle East is appreciated mainly for its shade and its ancient associations.

(CASHEW FAMILY—*ANACARDIACEAE*)

Pistacia Terebinthus.

FIG

Ficus carica

And when the woman saw that the tree was good for food, and that it was pleasant to the eyes, and a tree to be desired to make one wise, she took of the fruit thereof, and did eat, and gave also unto her husband with her and he did eat.
And the eyes of them both were opened, and they knew that they were naked and they sewed fig leaves together, and made themselves aprons.

(GENESIS 3: 6–7)

While it isn't clear what *fruit* was eaten in the Adam and Eve story, there is no doubt about the identity of the leaves with which the guilty couple covered themselves. And fig leaves have been appearing artistically in this context ever since. Mentioned more than fifty times in the Bible, the fig tree, like the vine, was clearly of great importance—being one of the 'seven species' with which the land of Israel was blessed—and symbolic of peace, prosperity and felicity:

For, lo, the winter is past, the rain is over and gone; the flowers appear on the earth; the time of the singing of birds is come, and the voice of the turtle is heard in our land; The fig tree putteth forth her green figs, and the vines with the tender grape give a good smell. Arise, my love, my fair one, and come away.

(SONG OF SOLOMON 2: 11–13)

People planted fig trees near their houses and enjoyed the shade and the feeling of security which they provided:

And Judah and Israel dwelt safely, every man under his vine and under his fig tree. . . .

(1 KINGS 4: 25)

The fruits, fresh and dried, have been prized since ancient times for their sweetness and their nutritional value. Botanically speaking it is a curiosity—its flowers are enclosed in the fleshy receptacle, which is not really a fruit; they never actually see the light of day yet nonetheless grow to perfection and ripen their seeds, the female flowers having been fertilised by a tiny fig-wasp, which brings pollen from the male flowers (on another fig tree) and enters the fleshy receptacle by a minute hole in the top. Figs are very nourishing and were used by Greek athletes to improve their performance. The Italians too have always been partial to them (figs were found in Pompeii), whilst the Romans boiled ham and bacon with the dried fruit and fattened pigs with them for a favourite gourmet dish of fig-flavoured liver. Nowadays Parma ham is served (deliciously) with fresh figs.

Dried fruits were important in medieval Britain too, especially during Lent when the rich enjoyed fish pies made with figs, raisins, apples, sugar and wine (there was no distinction then between sweet and savoury dishes). The association of dried fruits with festive occasions such as Christmas still persists (figgy pudding, for example). You can buy figs fresh, dried, or in tins according to season, and the best dried ones come from Lerida in Catalonia—rich brown and with thin skins. Tinned ones make a good instant dessert, sprinkled with *anisette* and served with cream.

In the Middle East, compôtes of dried fruits are popular. Soak dried apricots, figs, prunes, and raisins overnight, then boil gently with a piece of cinnamon and serve cold sprinkled with lemon juice and rose- or orange-flower water.

Medicinally, figs are used mainly for their mild laxative action, though Culpeper (17th century) recommends using the latex from the stems for the removal of warts. I am not sure that I would recommend *this* however, as the substance is now known to cause irritation of the skin.

FIG PUDDING
(Mrs Beeton)

1 kg (2 lb) dried figs
500 g (1 lb) suet
250 g (½ lb) flour
250 g (½ lb) breadcrumbs
2 eggs
milk

Cut the figs into small pieces, grate the bread finely, and chop the suet very small; mix these well together, add the flour, the eggs, which should be well beaten, and sufficient milk to form the whole into a stiff paste; butter a mould or basin, press the pudding into it very closely, tie it down with a cloth, and boil for three hours, or rather longer; turn it out of the mould, and serve with melted butter, wine-sauce, or cream.

URTICACEAE   DCLIX.

1329 *Ficus Carica L.*

(MULBERRY FAMILY—*MORACEAE*)

FIR

(Cilician fir) *Abies cilicica*

Fir trees—defined in my dictionary as 'any pyramidical coniferous tree of the northern temperate genus *Abies*, or any of the various other trees of the family *Pinaceae*, e.g. Douglas fir'—crop up frequently in the Scriptures, mostly in the building or ship-building context.

> *I will do [said Hiram of Tyre to Solomon] all thy desire concerning timber of cedar, and concerning timber of fir.*
>
> (1 KINGS 5: 8)

This wood was prized for even more specialised purposes than rafters or furniture or ships:

> *And David and all the house of Israel played before the LORD on all manner of instruments made of fir wood, even on harps, and on psalteries, and on timbrels, and on cornets, and on cymbals.*
>
> (2 SAMUEL 6: 5)

And well into the 18th century, the famous Dr Burney was reporting in his HISTORY OF MUSIC the continuing use of fir wood in instrument-making:

> *This species of wood, so soft in its nature, and sonorous in its effects, seems to have been preferred by the ancients, as well as moderns, to every other kind for the construction of musical instruments, particularly the bellies of them, on which their tone chiefly depends. Those of the harp, lute, guitar, harpsichord and violin, in present use, are constantly made of this wood.*

Fir trees still grow with cedars in mixed forests in Lebanon as they did at the time of Solomon's negotiations with Hiram, and the fir in question would have been the Cilician fir, though there are nearly forty species of *Abies* throughout the world. They have been put to much the same use over the centuries as pine trees. Firs also produce tar and pitch which was used in ship-building, also turpentine used for medicine and as a paint-drier.

A near relative of the fir is the spruce (*Picea abies*) of which there are numerous species, none of which however is found in Bible lands. 'It is of a mollifying, healing, and cleansing nature' says Culpeper (1649) of the 'fir tree', and he stresses its importance as an antiscorbutic, particularly for sailors whose diet makes them susceptible to scurvy.

You can make spruce beer by substituting the young branches and cones for hops and although I personally find the flavour a little medicinal, I have never had trouble persuading friends to partake of it. I make it with *Picea abies*, or Norway Spruce.

SPRUCE BEER
(A Country Cup)

a large panful of young spruce branches and cones
1 kg (2 lb) malt extract
12 l (2½ gals) water
25 g (1 oz) dried yeast

Boil the spruce in the water for about an hour (it smells marvellous!). Strain onto the malt in a large crock. Stir until dissolved and when tepid sprinkle over the dried yeast. Cover and leave to ferment for a few days, stirring from time to time. Syphon off into screw-top bottles after about 2 weeks, and leave until clear.

FIG. 14.—*ABIES CILICICA.*

a, part of spray, upper surface ; *b*, winter buds, non-resinous ; *c*, under-surface of leaf and pubescent shoot ; *d*, leaf in section, showing marginal resin canals.

(PINE FAMILY—*PINACEAE*)

FLAX

Linum usitatissimum

And the flax and the barley was smitten: for the barley was in the ear, and the flax was bolled.

(EXODUS 9: 31)

The seventh plague of Egypt was one of hail, 'which smote every herb of the field, and brake every tree of the field,' and ruined the flax and barley crops which were already mature and just about to be gathered. This was a great disaster, because flax, like barley, was an important crop, and had been so for some 5,000 years before the birth of Christ. Egyptian linen was celebrated from earliest times and though coarse by our standards, if we judge it by the cloths used to wrap the mummies, it was the chief material for clothing as well as for bedding, sails, fishing nets, ropes, threads and lampwicks.

Priests wore linen, and the body of Christ was wound 'in linen clothes with the spices, as the manner of the Jews is to bury' (JOHN 19: 40). There were various rules and prohibitions concerning it:

Thou shalt not wear a garment of divers sorts, as of woollen and linen together.

(DEUTERONOMY 22: 11)

Flax was important in the religious context. Linen has an inherent coolness—you can easily tell the difference between a cotton and a linen sheet by putting the fabric to your cheek—so for priests it was a pure material for ritual and ceremony:

When they enter in at the gates of the inner court, they shall be clothed with linen garments; and no wool shall come upon them ... they shall have linen bonnets upon their heads, and shall have linen breeches upon their loins; they shall not gird themselves with any thing that causeth sweat.

(EZEKIEL 44: 17, 18)

Flax is a pretty blue-flowered annual which is cultivated in many tropical and temperate areas. Besides the uses for the fibres, it is an important medicinal herb. The seeds are used, those from England and Holland being considered the finest. Linseed tea is good for urinary infections and constipation, and poultices of the crushed seeds are prescribed for both external and internal conditions, such as skin irritations and abscesses, bronchitis, neuritis and muscular pains. Linseed oil which is extracted from the seeds (the 'cake' which is left after this process is used to fatten cattle) is used in the manufacture of paints and varnishes (not to mention linoleum) and is extensively used by artists for its quick-drying properties. Some people mix it with honey as a face lotion to improve the complexion.

For a soothing, sedative bath which will soften the skin, boil 50 g (2oz) of the seeds for 2 minutes in a quart of water, and add to the bath.

Gerard's HERBALL has another suggestion for linseed: 'Being taken largely with pepper and honie made up into a cake, it stirreth up lust.'

Linen as a fabric has lately enjoyed a revival. It looks good, feels good and has only one drawback—it is easily creased and difficult to iron.

Linum usitatissimum

(FLAX FAMILY—*LINACEAE*)

FRANKINCENSE

Boswellia sacra, Boswellia thurifera

When they saw the star, they rejoiced with exceeding great joy.
And when they were come into the house, they saw the young child with
Mary his mother, and fell down, and worshipped him: and when they had
opened their treasures, they presented unto him gifts; gold, and frankincense,
and myrrh.

(MATTHEW 2: 10–11)

These were the mystical gifts of the Magi, and while most people understand that myrrh and frankincense, like gold, are rare and precious commodities, it is not generally known that they derive from plants, and are both resins which exude from the twigs and stems of shrubby Arabian trees.

Frankincense, or olibanum, as the drug is known in medicine, is practically synonymous with incense, of which it has always been a major ingredient (the Roman Catholic Church uses it extensively) but it is also used in perfumery and medicine. To obtain larger quantities than occur naturally, an incision is made in the trunk and a narrow piece of bark stripped off. The milk-like juice which exudes forms shiny, yellow or pinkish 'tears' when exposed to the air for about three months, and these are then scraped off and collected in baskets. The Bedouins gather frankincense and other gums and resins between May and September before the first rain and it was an important item of commerce between Arabia and Israel in biblical times, being one of the four 'sweet scents' of the Jewish ceremonial incense. It was well-known in a secular context too:

Who is this that cometh out of the wilderness like pillars of smoke, perfumed
with myrrh and frankincense, *with all powders of the merchant?*

(SONG OF SOLOMON 3: 6)

Charred frankincense was one of the substances used for the making of kohl for painting the eyes. Jezebel probably used it before her dreadful end:

. . . she painted her face, and tired her head, and looked out at a window.

(2 KINGS 9: 30)

This practise of beautifying the eyes is referred to as well, in JEREMIAH 4: 30:

Though thou clothest thyself with crimson, though thou deckest thee with
ornaments of gold, though thou rentest thy face with painting, in vain shall
thou make thyself fair; thy lovers will despise thee, they will seek thy life.

Burnt almond shells, powdered lead and antimony were similarly used—by men as well as women—as you can see from the sculptures and paintings in the temples and tombs of ancient Egypt.

There was some supposed medicinal property in kohl and Gerard's HERBALL recommends frankincense to drive away 'the dimnes of the eyesight'. Egyptian women used it, melted, as a depilatory which sounds a more reliable method than the primitive one to which Edward Lane refers, in his ACCOUNT OF THE MANNERS AND CUSTOMS OF THE MODERN EGYPTIANS written in the first part of the 19th century:

by applying the blood of a bat to the skin of a newly-born female infant, on the parts where they wish no hair to grow, they assert that they accomplish this desire.

Frankincense was also chewed to sweeten the breath, but its main use was, and is, as an ingredient of incense. You can buy frankincense at good herbalists and it is not as expensive as you might imagine. Here, then, are two recipes to experiment with.

INCENSE (1)
275 g (10 oz) olibanum (Frankincense)
110 g (4 oz) benzoin
110 g (4 oz) storax

Break into little pieces, mix.

INCENSE (2)
1 part myrrh
5 parts frankincense
2½ parts benzoin

Mix, and burn on charcoal.

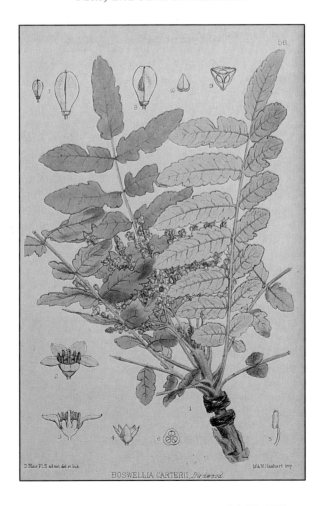

BOSWELLIA CARTERII *Birdwood.*

(FRANKINCENSE FAMILY—*BURSERACEAE*)

GALBANUM

Ferula gummosa

And the LORD said unto Moses, Take unto thee sweet spices, stacte, and onycha, and galbanum; these sweet spices with pure frankincense: of each shall there be a like weight: And thou shalt make it a perfume, a confection after the art of the apothecary, tempered together, pure and holy.

(EXODUS 30: 34–35)

Like cassia and cinnamon and other ingredients of the holy oils and incenses used by the Israelites, galbanum must have been imported (probably from Persia), as the plant which produces it did not grow in ancient Israel or in any of its neighbouring countries. It is a gum resin from a giant fennel-like plant which Gerard calls *Herbe ferula* or *Fennell Gyant*. He had it growing in his garden near London where it reached the remarkable height of 14 to 15 feet—much greater than 'from whence it came'—due to the moister English climate. The stem of the plant exudes a milky juice which solidifies to form a bitter aromatic gum—and incisions are made in the rootstock to release more of the fluid. This substance, known as 'tears' in the trade, is the commercial galbanum, and a somewhat rare commodity. It used to be quite important medicinally and the Greek physician and physiologist Galen (2nd century A.D.) recommends its astringent properties. Like other exotic substances, it was also reported that Ferula had aphrodisiac qualities:

> *. . . rosted in the embers, first wrapped in leaves or in old clouts, with pepper and salt, which as they say, is a pleasant sweete foode, that stirreth up lust . . .*
>
> (*Gerard's* HERBALL)

Galbanum produces a volatile oil of a fine indigo blue which can be used as a stimulant, as an expectorant in chronic bronchitis and as a carminative. Gerard gives a lengthy list of its virtues in his HERBALL, and recommends it for almost every ailment from coughs and cramps to tumours and broken bones—not to mention the pains of childbirth!

> *It helpeth womens painfull travell, if they do take thereof in a cup of wine the quantitie of a beane.*

The smoke has a strong and piercing smell and was believed to drive away serpents. It was used in incense preparations. Of the ingredients quoted in Moses' recipe above, stacte is generally considered to be the resin of *Styrax officinalis* or the gum of *Liquidambar orientalis*, and frankincense a resin from the shrub *Boswellia*. Onycha is less certain. It is believed to be either a gum or perfume, or the deliciously fragrant essence obtained from the shell of a small mollusc from the Red Sea. Galbanum still features in the BRITISH PHARMACEUTICAL CODEX. It is employed as a stimulant and expectorant in chronic bronchitis and is usually administered in pill form because of its bitter taste.

(CARROT FAMILY—*UMBELLIFERAE*)

FERULA GALBANIFLUA, *Boiss & Buhse.*

GARLIC

Allium sativum

*We remember the fish, which we did eat in Egypt freely; the cucumbers, and
the melons, and the leeks, and the onions, and the* garlick.

(NUMBERS 11: 5)

Here are the Israelites of the Exodus tiring of their monotonous diet of manna, and
yearning for favourite foods. Leeks, onions and garlic have been extensively
cultivated since ancient times and are of course still basic and important vegetables in
Middle Eastern cookery. All three are members of the same genus in the large lily family,
but garlic is in a class of its own. It is not just the smell, which is uniquely pungent—
some might say rank—but also its medicinal and health-giving properties, which were, and
are, greatly esteemed. Such qualities are not stressed in the Scriptures, needless to say, as
references to the healing powers of plants would surely detract from belief in God's all-
embracing divine power. But herbs were certainly used medicinally in biblical times, and
are so today, by the peasant and Bedouin. There is a record too of large quantities of
garlic having been supplied to the labourers building the great Pyramid of Cheops. Many
people believe that daily garlic gives strength and protects from disease and it has its
place in our modern pharmacopoeias for its antiseptic, diaphoretic, diuretic and
expectorant qualities. You can take it in syrup or capsule form, because there is always
the problem of the lingering after-effects on the breath. In Jordan, people chew cardamom
seeds for this, and on the Continent parsley, apple or aniseed are recommended.

The Romans brought garlic to Britain with other favourite condiments, and it was
universally appreciated in medieval times by rich and poor alike. During Elizabeth I's
reign it was known as 'poor man's physick' and sailors took it to sea because 'it pacifieth
the disposition to vomit'. Gradually however, it went out of favour, eventually becoming
unacceptable in polite circles. It was even proscribed by the enlightened John Evelyn in
his fresh and 'modern' ACETARIA, A DISCOURSE OF SALLETS in 1699:

> *We absolutely forbid it entrance into our salleting, by reason of its intolerable
> rankness. To be sure, 'tis not for ladies palats, nor those who court them. . . .*

Mrs Beeton too dismisses garlic as 'the most acrimonious in its taste of the whole of the
alliaceous tribe.' But things have changed now, and in Britain and North America garlic
is acceptable in most circles (polite or otherwise) thanks to the absorption of new tastes
and cookery introduced by immigrants from Asia and Europe.

I highly recommend that wonderful Provençal dish *Aioli*—which is basically a garlic
(very!) flavoured mayonnaise served with fish or hard-boiled eggs, snails, poached chicken
or lightly boiled vegetables. You make the mayonnaise in the usual way, but start off
with 4 crushed cloves of garlic for 2 egg yolks and about 500 ml ($\frac{1}{2}$ pt) of olive oil. If a
subtler effect is wanted, rub a cut clove round the salad bowl before putting in the
dressing, and always bear in mind that long cooking makes its taste milder.

Gerard in his HERBALL recommends garlic for coughs, sore throats and for wind and
here is a later writer, Sir John Harington, whose ENGLISHMAN'S DOCTOR of 1609 is composed
in quatrains:

Sith Garlicke then hath power to save from death,
Beare with it though it makes unsavoury breath;
And scorne not Garlicke, like to some that think
it onely makes men winke, and drinke, and stinke.

(LILY FAMILY—*LILIACEAE*)

GOURD

(Castor oil plant) *Ricinus communis*

And the LORD God prepared a gourd, and made it to come up over Jonah, that it might be a shadow over his head, to deliver him from his grief. So Jonah was exceeding glad of the gourd. But God prepared a worm when the morning rose the next day, and it smote the gourd that it withered.

(JONAH 4: 6–7)

Scholars have come to blows, it is reported, over the true identity of the plant which God provided for Jonah's temporary shelter—Augustine and Jerome to be precise—the former accusing Jerome of heresy when he insisted that it was ivy and not a gourd at all. It is now accepted that it was neither, and that the rapid-growing castor oil plant was the one in question. It grows to twelve feet or more and produces a large number of palmate leaves which would have provided admirable shelter for Jonah. Although Jonah's plant with which he was so pleased was not a gourd, the true wild gourd is mentioned in the Bible (see page 146). *Palma Christi* is another name for the castor oil plant and the seeds have been found in 6,000-year-old Egyptian tombs according to Michael Zohary's book, PLANTS OF THE BIBLE. Dioscorides, physician to Antony and Cleopatra and author of a book on medicinal herbs, describes it and mentions the oil which is expressed from the seeds. This is the well-known or dreaded castor oil with which we were threatened as children—a sure cure for constipation and of an acrid and nauseous taste. This oil was known to the Hebrews, who used it widely in their ceremonial rites, and its medicinal properties are mentioned in the TALMUD. Castor oil still features in the BRITISH PHARMACEUTICAL CODEX (*B.P.C.*) as a mild purgative suitable for children and old people, but it is rather unfashionable now as it can cause sickness. Castor oil is more popular these days in ophthalmic medicine and can soothe irritation in the eye after the removal of a foreign body. Industrially too, it is used for manufacturing transparent soap, as a lubricant for aircraft engines, clocks and watches, and in plastics and varnishes.

The seeds, on the other hand, are violently purgative due to the presence of the highly toxic substance *ricin*, and as few as three seeds have been known to kill an adult. In the 16th century they were administered in fairly drastic cases:

> Ricinus *his seede taken inwardly, openeth the bellie, and causeth vomit, drawing slimie flegme and choler from the places possessed therewith.*
>
> (*Gerard's* HERBALL, *1597*)

And the oil was recommended 'to annoint and rub all rough hardnes and scurvinesse gotten by itch.'

Italy produces the best castor oil from seeds grown in the countryside around Verona and it is used cosmetically and in hair lotions as well as medicinally. You can buy a special deodorant castor oil for this purpose.

Here is an Italian recipe for a brilliantine to strengthen the hair:

BRILLIANTINE
20 g ($\frac{3}{4}$ oz) castor oil
15 g ($\frac{1}{2}$ oz) olive oil
20 g ($\frac{3}{4}$ oz) eau de cologne

Mix together and use once a day to make the hair shine, to prevent dandruff and to strengthen the roots.[9]

The plant was well known in English gardens (as well as on the Continent) in the mid-16th century, and it can be easily grown from seed. Sow them in March but keep the young plants under glass until June. In their native countries they are perennial, but they don't normally survive the winter in colder climates. They are handsome and striking plants and given plenty of water will grow to a good size.

Castor oil, by the way, used to be sold in Scotland in tall elegant bottles of a beautiful blue, and these are rare and valuable collectors' items now.

(SPURGE FAMILY—*EUPHORBIACEAE*)

HEATH

(Juniper) *Juniperus*

Thus saith the LORD; Cursed be the man that trusteth in man, and maketh flesh his arm, and whose heart departeth from the LORD. For he shall be like the heath *in the desert, and shall not see when good cometh; but shall inhabit the parched places in the wilderness, in a salt land and not inhabited.*

(JEREMIAH 17: 5–6)

When juniper occurs in the Scriptures it is now accepted that the plant is in fact broom, and to confuse the issue when heath is mentioned the plant in question is believed to be juniper! It is not a true desert tree in the way that the carob is, but is nonetheless believed to have occurred in isolated stands in desert regions during biblical times.

There are about 60 species of juniper and the *Phoenician* is the likeliest in this context. It doesn't normally exceed 14 or 15 feet in height and can live for several hundred years.

Flee, save your lives, and be like the heath *in the wilderness. For because thou hast trusted in thy works and in thy treasures, thou shalt also be taken: and Chemosh shall go forth into captivity with his priests and his princes together.*

(JEREMIAH 48: 6–7)

Heath, or juniper, is despised and rejected here. But the plant, or rather the berries—in particular of *Juniperus communis*—have proved their value over the centuries, and not only as a flavouring for gin. The Elizabethans put the juice of juniper berries in *aqua vitae* or *aqua compositae* and around the same time the Dutch were using juniper to flavour the corn spirits which were beginning to oust brandy wine. The British were quick to appreciate this new product and were soon importing it under the name of genever or gin.

'The berries . . . procure appetite when it is lost . . .' wrote Culpeper in 1649, and gin and tonic is a classic aperitif in Britain. In North America, gin with a green olive, a tiny measure of vermouth and ice in a chilled glass makes up the classic dry martini. 'Mother's ruin', as gin was called because of its damaging effects on the family life of the poor in the 18th century (before taxation pushed up the price), is the basis of many of our modern cocktails and in pre-anaesthesia days its stupefying effects were utilised in the operating theatre.

In the kitchen, juniper berries are of great culinary interest and are used in marinades and court-bouillons, pâtés, game dishes and so on. Aromatic and resinous, juniper is also used in perfumes and colognes, and the wood used to be burned in times of plague or cholera epidemics to fumigate houses and people.

Oil of juniper is used medicinally as a diuretic and carminative and more often in veterinary medicine but you can also use it in pot-pourri.

DRY MARTINI
four or five parts dry gin
one part vermouth

Stir with ice and strain into chilled glass. Serve with twist of lemon peel or an olive.

1142. nana W.

1141 *Juniperus communis* L.

(CYPRESS FAMILY—*CUPRESSACEAE*)

HEMLOCK
Conium maculatum

My heart aches, and a drowsy numbness pains
My sense, as though of hemlock I had drunk,
Or emptied some dull opiate to the drains
One minute past, and Lethe-wards had sunk: . . .

This was Keats in 'Ode to a Nightingale,' and hemlock was the poison which killed Socrates. But the symptoms are somewhat less poetic—rolling of the eyes, salivation, bloating, laboured breathing and finally complete paralysis with the mind remaining clear to the end.

The drug coniine, which is a liquid alkaloid obtained from all parts of the plant, appears in the BRITISH PHARMACOPOEIA and its depressant action has been used in the treatment of cholera, mania, paralysis agitans, tetanus and strychnine poisoning.

In the Bible hemlock appears only twice (in AMOS 6: 12 and HOSEA 10: 4) and the Hebrew word (*rosh*) is more often translated as *gall*:

For their vine is of the vine of Sodom, and of the fields of Gomorrah: their grapes are grapes of gall, their clusters are bitter.

(DEUTERONOMY 32: 32)

The same gall was offered to Christ on the cross:

And when they were come unto a place called Golgotha, that is to say, a place of a skull, they gave him vinegar to drink mingled with gall: and when he had tasted thereof, he would not drink.

(MATTHEW 27: 33–34)

Belying its deadly qualities with its grace, hemlock does however give warning signals with its fetid, mouse-like odour and the ominous purple blotching on its stem (to which its specific name *maculatum* refers). It is a moisture-loving plant, native and abundant in Europe and introduced to North America. It grows by the sides of streams and rivers and is often confused with other umbelliferous plants like wild chervil (*Anthriscus sylvestris*) and fool's parsley (*Aethusa cynapium*). It loses most of its poisonous properties on drying, but children have been poisoned by making whistles out of the hollow stems. In cases of coniine poisoning the stomach must be emptied, stimulants applied and an antidote of tannic acid given.

The sedative qualities of hemlock have been used externally too, for the relief of pain, but in Gerard's HERBALL there is a warning against external use with reference to a bizarre practice:

It is therefore a very rash part to laie the leaves of Homlockes to the stones of yoong boies or virgins brests, and by that meanes to keepe those parts from growing great: for it doth not onely easely cause those members to pine away, but also hurteth the hart and liver. . . .

76

Gerard dismisses the plant altogether from medicinal use declaring that it possesses no positive faculties to be used in 'physick':

Hemlocke *is a very evill, dangerous, hurtfull, and poysonous herbe, insomuch that whosoever taketh of it into his body dieth remedilesse . . .*

Such qualities were certainly known in biblical times and hemlock is thus used metaphorically and to denote all kinds of poison:

Remembering mine affliction and my misery, the wormwood and the gall. *My soul hath them still in remembrance, and is humbled in me.*

(LAMENTATIONS 3: 19–20)

Conium maculatum

(CARROT FAMILY—*UMBELLIFERAE*)

HYSSOP

Hyssopus officinalis
(Syrian hyssop or white marjoram)
Origanum syriacum

Purge me with hyssop, *and I shall be clean: wash me, and I shall be whiter than snow.*

(PSALM 51: 7)

The Hebrew word is *ezov*, and actually does not mean so much a specific plant, but something which can be tied up in bunches and used for cleansing ceremonies. It is frequently mentioned in the Bible in a context of ritual purification and sacrifice, particularly for the Passover; and *hyssop* is generally understood:

Then Moses called for all the elders of Israel, and said unto them, Draw out and take you a lamb according to your families, and kill the passover. And ye shall take a bunch of hyssop, *and dip it in the blood that is in the bason, and strike the lintel and the two side posts with the blood that is in the bason; and none of you shall go out at the door of his house until the morning.*

(EXODUS 12: 21–22)

But it figures too in 'the law of the leper in the day of his cleansing. . . .' (LEVITICUS 14: 4, 6) along with cedar wood and scarlet (a bright red dye obtained from insects living on the kermes oak).

Hyssopus officinalis is an evergreen semi-shrub native to southern Europe and common in the stony soil of the sunny Mediterranean, but it has long been cultivated as a medicinal, aromatic and ornamental plant, although it is not found in Israel or Sinai. The Romans introduced it into Britain with other herbs such as parsley, rosemary, savory and marjoram, and it became popular especially in the Middle Ages for flavouring roast meats, soups and stuffings. In the 18th and 19th centuries tainted fish would be gutted, laid on dry rushes and covered with hyssop in order to 'rescue' it, and when herb beers became popular in the north of England hyssop was one of the several plants used for flavouring. The nauseous flavour of raw crude spirits like absinthe, too, was tempered by the addition of hyssop, wormwood and mint. Nowadays, it is rarely used for flavouring food because of its rather strong taste (its pungency made it a popular strewing herb) but it is still valued medicinally, and hyssop tea is a well-tried European country remedy for rheumatism and complaints of the respiratory tract.

Syrian hyssop (Origanum syriacum), which is probably the one referred to in EXODUS, as it grows abundantly in Israel and Sinai, is still used by the Arabs in cookery and for tea. The hairs on its stems are said to prevent the coagulation of blood—hence, probably, its use in passover rituals. Hyssop features in the *New Testament* too:

Now there was set a vessel full of vinegar: and they filled a spunge with vinegar, and put it upon hyssop, *and put it to his mouth. When Jesus therefore had received the vinegar, he said, It is finished: and he bowed his head, and gave up the ghost.*

(JOHN 19: 28–30)

So hyssop, according to the Gospel of St John, the pungent herb of purification was used to flavour Christ's last drink of vinegar, or sour wine, given to him compassionately on the cross.

Hyssopus officinalis is an attractive plant which may be grown in most sunny situations. It is a favourite of honey bees who work its flowers for nectar and pollen.

Origanum Maru

(MINT FAMILY—*LABIATAE*)

JUNIPER

(Broom) *Retama raetam*

But he himself went a day's journey into the wilderness, and came and sat down under a juniper tree: and he requested for himself that he might die; and said, It is enough; now, O LORD, take away my life; for I am not better than my fathers. And as he lay and slept under a juniper tree, behold, then an angel touched him, and said unto him, Arise and eat.

(1 KINGS 19: 4–5)

*R*othem is the Hebrew word (mistranslated above as juniper) which corresponds to the Arabic *ratam* which is a type of broom common in the deserts of Israel, Arabia and the Sahara. The shade of this pretty white-flowered shrub could hardly be described as luxuriant, but in the treeless desert it would be welcome enough. The white broom is also a native of Sicily, Arabia, the Sahara and other hot regions, and the roots were used as fuel too. Probably this is what Job refers to rather than to a diet of broom, which would be hard indeed:

For want and famine they were solitary; fleeing into the wilderness in former time desolate and waste. Who cut up mallows by the bushes, and juniper roots for their meat....

(JOB 30: 3–4)

The following quotation from PSALM 120 refers to the fact that *Retama* wood gives the fiercest fire of any combustible matter to be found in the desert, and thus the most fitting punishment for a deceitful tongue!

What shall be given unto thee? or what shall be done unto thee, thou false tongue? Sharp arrows of the mighty, with coals of juniper....

(PSALM 120: 3–4)

Broom was used for warmth as well as for cooking, as it could be extremely cold in the desert at night, and the Greek herbalist Dioscorides mentions also the parasite *Orobanche* or broomrape which grows on the roots of broom and could be eaten fresh or boiled like asparagus. This was used medicinally too:

The rape of the Broome or Broome Rape, being boyled in wine, is commended against the pains of the kidneies and bladder, provoketh urine, breaketh the stone, and expelleth it.

(*Gerard's* HERBALL, *1597*)

There is a myth concerning broom which varies according to its country of origin. One version tells that when Mary and Joseph fled into Egypt the Virgin cursed the broom because its ripe pods crackled as they passed and so they risked discovery by Herod's soldiers. Another tells how during the flight to Egypt all the plants drew back and spread their branches wide to make a path for the Virgin—except the broom, which remained stiff and unyielding, and so it is condemned to remain so. It is this unbending quality which makes for excellent broomsticks and legend has it that medieval witches used them for their nocturnal flights.

Broom is a good beekeeper's plant too. It is pollinated by bees, and all varieties, both native and cultivated, are well worked by them for pollen and nectar.

Flora Danica Tab DCVIII:

(PEA FAMILY—*LEGUMINOSAE*)

LEEK

Allium porrum

*We remember the fish, which we did eat in Egypt freely; the cucumbers, and
the melons, and the* leeks, *and the onions, and the garlick: But now our soul
is dried away: there is nothing at all, beside this manna, before our eyes.*

(NUMBERS 11: 5–6)

It is scarcely surprising that the Hebrews longed for these three members of the Lily
family, leeks, onions and garlic, as they must all have been important articles of diet
then, as they are now. Leeks were well known in ancient Egypt and were valued not only
for food but for medicinal use—they were used to treat burns. Pliny, writing in the 1st
century A.D. describes how the Emperor Nero ate leeks 'for certaine daies in every moneth
for to scoure his throat, and cleare his voice, and to take it with oile; on which daies he
did eat nothing else, not so much as bread.' Leeks, in quantity, were prescribed for infertile
women and have traditionally been used internally and externally for a variety of
conditions. 'The Leeke is hot and dry, and doth attenuate or make thinne as doth the
Onion,' writes Gerard, and leek broth is prescribed not only for obesity but for kidney
complaints, intestinal disorders and coughs. When a child swallows a sharp object such as
a nail, boiled leeks should be given as soon after the incident as possible and continued
until the object is expelled in the normal way. The fibres sheathe the sharp point and so
protect the stomach and bowel from perforation.

From a culinary point of view the leek is an extremely versatile and useful vegetable,
both in its own right and as a flavouring agent in other dishes. It has a more delicate
flavour then garlic or onion, and forms the basis of many classic European, North
American and Middle-Eastern dishes. Leeks make exquisite soups such as the famous
vichyssoise, the French *soupe à la bonne femme* and the old Scots soup cock-a-leekie. They
were useful Lenten fare in Britain during the spring 'hungry-gap':

> *Now leeks are in season, for pottage full good,*
> *and spareth the milchcow, and purgeth the blood:*
> *These having with peason, for pottage in Lent,*
> *thou sparest both oatmeal and bread to be spent.*
> (FIVE HUNDRETH POINTES OF GOOD HUSBANDRIE . . . NEWLIE AUGMENTED,
> *Thomas Tusser, 1590*)

The gentry enjoyed them in medieval times in white *porray* (from the Latin *porrum*)
which was a purée of the white part of the vegetable, mixed with rice and almond milk
and sweetened with honey. Sometimes the *porray* was based on a meat broth or ham
stock and reinforced by pieces of meat or small birds.

Hasselquist, in VOYAGES AND TRAVELS IN THE LEVANT (1766), writes that the Arabians
'are very fond of eating leeks, raw as sauce for their roasted meat; and the poor people eat
it raw with their bread, especially for breakfast.' Nowadays, even for salads, they tend to
be lightly cooked before being dressed with oil and vinegar.

I haven't a bad word to say of the noble leek, but of its 'hurts' Gerard has this to say
in the HERBALL of 1597:

It heateth the bodie, ingendreth naughtie blood, causeth troublesome and terrible dreames, offendeth the eies, dulleth the sight, hurteth those that are by nature hot and cholericke, and is noisome to the stomacke, and breedeth windines.

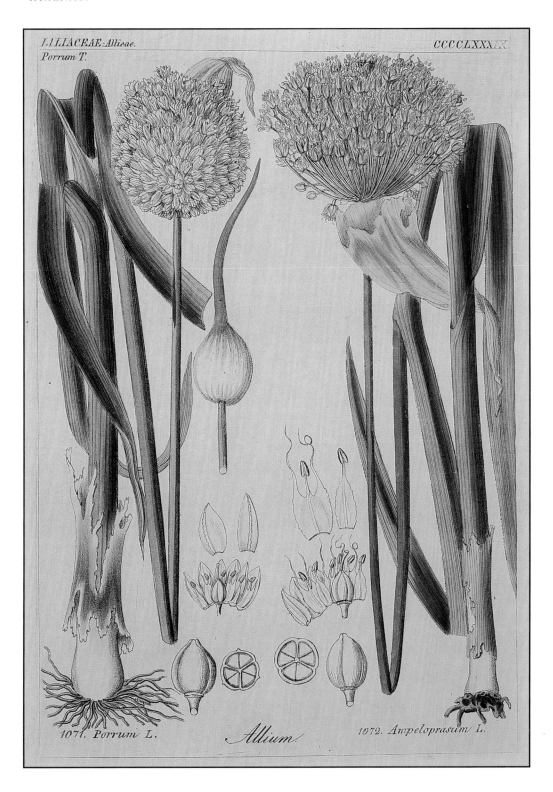

(LILY FAMILY—*LILIACEAE*)

LENTIL

Lens culinaris

And Jacob sod pottage: and Esau came from the field, and he was faint: And Esau said to Jacob, Feed me, I pray thee, with that same red pottage; for I am faint: therefore was his name called Edom. And Jacob said, Sell me this day thy birthright. And Esau said, Behold, I am at the point to die: and what profit shall this birthright do to me? And Jacob said, Swear to me this day; and he sware unto him: and he sold his birthright unto Jacob. Then Jacob gave Esau bread and pottage of lentiles: *and he did eat and drink, and rose up, and went his way: thus Esau despised his birthright.*

(GENESIS 25: 29–34)

Lentils were an important crop in ancient Israel and today Jews and Arabs alike continue to enjoy the soup for which Esau sold his birthright. It was probably composed of red lentils with onions, carrots and meat such as lamb, or more probably venison in the case of Esau, since he was a hunter. But there are many variations and yellow, green or brown lentils can be used—the latter will not disintegrate in the cooking. Meat can be omitted, and strips of sautéd spinach or garlic croûtons make a delicious addition.

Lentils are highly nutritious, containing iron and vitamin B and, like the other pulses, are very versatile and a useful source of protein for vegetarians. They can also be dried and ground into flour for a coarse bread with other pulses and grains:

Take thou also unto thee wheat, and barley, and beans, and lentiles, *and millet, and fitches, and put them in one vessel, and make thee bread thereof. . . .*

(EZEKIEL 4: 9)

Lentil flour is still made into bread by the very poor in parts of the Middle East. Even in Britain, where lentils used to be grown in a few places for fodder, it was used to make a coarse but hearty bread in the 17th and 18th centuries. Peas and beans were similarly used, and the latter was probably the least palatable of all breads, brittle and impossible to form into loaves. Lentils were well-known in Gerard's day in Europe. He grew them in his garden and reports that they were sown for cattle feed around Watford and attributes powerful medicinal properties to them:

The meale of Lentiles *mixed with honie, doth mundifie and clense corrupt ulcers and rotten sores, filling them with flesh againe and is most singular to be put into the common digestives used among our London Chirurgians [surgeons] for greene wounds.*

(*Gerard's* HERBALL, *1597*)

But they had their drawbacks too, apparently, and could cause troublesome dreams, were bad for the head, sinews and lungs, and 'a most dangerous food for dry and withered bodies.' Lentils are no longer used medicinally but are greatly valued for their nourishment. If they *do* have a drawback it is their tendency to cause wind!

(PEA FAMILY—*LEGUMINOSAE*)

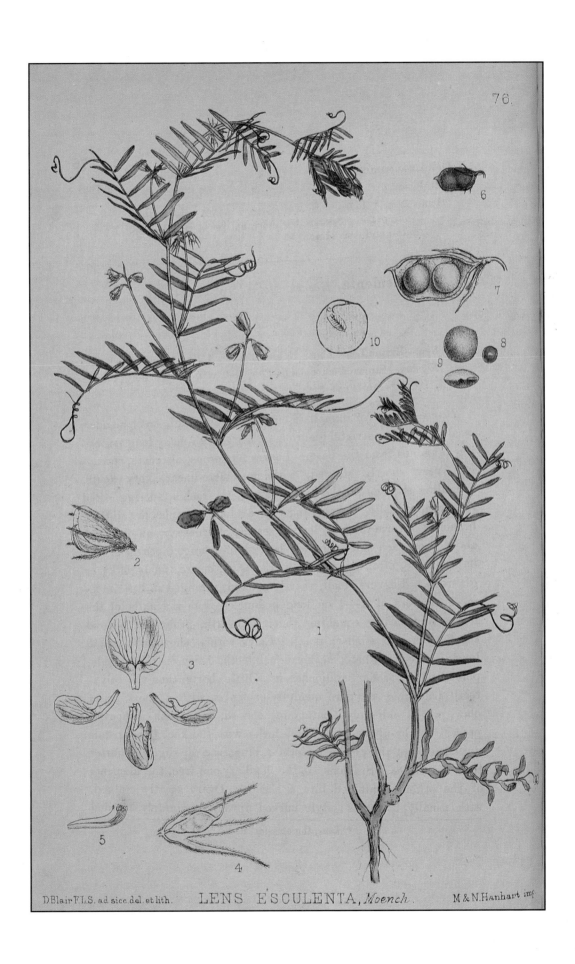

D.Blair F.L.S. ad sicc.del.et lith. LENS ESCULENTA, *Moench*. M & N.Hanhart imp

LILY

Lilium candidum

I am the rose of Sharon, and the lily *of the valleys. As the* lily *among thorns, so is my love among the daughters.*

(SONG OF SOLOMON 2: 1–2)

A flower of exquisite beauty, *Lilium candidum* has come to represent purity and innocence, and is frequently associated with the Virgin Mary, herself a symbol of purity. It is the lily of the valley of SONG OF SOLOMON and often features in religious painting (Botticelli, Titian and Memling for example), is used to decorate churches on special occasions and is sometimes called the Madonna lily. The Greeks called it the 'Flower of Flowers' and according to classical mythology its colour was changed from purple to purest white by a drop of milk spilled from Juno's breast when her brother (and husband) Jupiter placed his son Hercules at her breast while she slept. Juno was queen of the heavens, protected cleanliness and presided over marriage and childbirth. The dittany, poppy and lily were her favourite flowers and in the old herbals *Lilium candidum* is called *Rosa Junonis* or Juno's Rose.

This flower has been the inspiration for much decorative art, not only the columns of Solomon's temple:

And the chapiters that were upon the top of the pillars were of lily *work in the porch, four cubits.*

(1 KINGS 7: 19)

but also in Assyrian art, Roman and Greek scroll work, and right throughout the history of art to the present day.

It is hardly surprising that a flower of such immaculate whiteness should have been used over the years to treat nature's blots and blemishes. Lily bulbs are recommended for boils, abscesses, corns, whitlows and for blotchiness of the skin, and extract of lily root forms the basis of some present day hand-creams and body lotions.

For wrinkles you should massage gently in circular motion with the juice of the bulb, and for a face lotion to beautify the skin, prepare Lily Water by boiling 120 grams of bulbs in half a litre of water until reduced by a third. In rural France, fresh petals are macerated in *eau de vie* for an antiseptic which promotes the healing of burns and sores. I must admit that given a supply of lilies I'd be loathe to do anything other than admire their beauty, which is a therapy in itself.

As for the lilies of the field:

And why take ye thought for raiment? Consider the lilies *of the field, how they grow; they toil not, neither do they spin: And yet I say unto you, That even Solomon in all his glory was not arrayed like one of these. Wherefore, if God so clothe the grass of the field, which to day is, and to morrow is cast into the oven, shall he not much more clothe you, O ye of little faith?*

(MATTHEW 6: 28–30)

Lilium Candidum   *Lis Blanc*

Lilies in this case simply means common wild flowers. *Lilium candidum* is a mountain plant (it grows on Mount Carmel and in Galilee) and so is not to be associated with the 'grass' or common herbage to which Christ refers. Poppies, chamomiles, tulips, narcissi, crowfoots and anemones provide spectacular colourful displays throughout spring and summer and in the *Old Testament* too they symbolise the ephemeral nature of things in contrast to the ever-enduring word of God.

> *. . . all flesh is grass, and all the goodliness thereof is as the* flower of the field: *The grass withereth, the flower fadeth . . . but the word of our God shall stand for ever.*
>
> (ISAIAH 40: 6–8)

(LILY FAMILY—*LILIACEAE*)

Papaver Rhœas.

MALLOW

Malva sylvestris

For want and famine they were solitary; fleeing into the wilderness in former time desolate and waste. Who cut up mallows by the bushes, and juniper roots for their meat.

(JOB 30: 3–4)

Although most scholars are agreed that mallow in this case does not refer to *Malva sylvestris* (which is not a desert plant) it is in all probability the one mentioned in JOB 6: 6–7, and translated 'white of an egg' in the *Authorised Version*:

Can that which is unsavoury be eaten without salt? or is there any taste in the white of an egg? The things that my soul refused to touch are as my sorrowful meat.

Mallow (*Malva sylvestris*) was greatly esteemed by the Greeks and Romans. Horace and Martial recommend it for developing the intellectual faculties and Pythagoras for moderating the passions and cleansing both stomach and mind. Cicero used a purge of mallow and beet stewed together, and Pliny declares that a spoonful of common mallow will protect from disease.

It figures importantly in modern Italian herbals for the treatment of arthritis and gout, abscesses, gingivitis, throat infections, obesity and severe toothache, and a mallow bath is recommended for nervous problems and to help promote a good night's sleep:

OLD ITALIAN RECIPE

Prepare a decoction of 3 litres of water and 30 g of leaves and flowers of mallow. Boil for 20 minutes. Add the strained liquid to the bath water and lie in it for a good quarter of an hour.

Children have used the leaves like dock to relieve the stings of nettles, and the fruits, which resemble cheeses, are eaten by them (they are called *fromages* in France).

> *The sitting down when school was oer*
> *Upon the threshold by his door*
> *Picking from mallows sport to please*
> *Each crumpld seed he calld a cheese.*
> (John Clare: 'May', in THE SHEPHERD'S CALENDAR)

In prehistoric times, mallows, along with nettles, docks and plantains, were added to the stewpot and this practice continued until at least the 17th century; a garden variety had been introduced by the Romans. More recently they were discarded because of their slimy texture, but it is this very quality which makes them a valuable basis for an emollient used for the treatment of acute inflammation of the respiratory, gastric and urinary tracts.

Although the medicinal use of *Malva sylvestris* has been greatly superseded by marsh mallow (*M. moschatus*), it is still employed by country people and an infusion of the leaves and flowers is a popular remedy for coughs and colds, while the leaves can be boiled as a wholesome vegetable. In the Middle East mallow leaves are still used to make a traditional soup called Melokhia.

The Mallow of JOB 30: 4 ('Who cut up mallows by the bushes, and juniper roots for their meat') is identified these days as the shrubby orache, *Atriplex halinus*. It is a common salt-tasting desert plant known to be used for food in times of scarcity. Other members of the orache family, *Atriplex hastata* and *Atriplex patula* are occasionally collected in Europe and North America by free-food foragers and they are good in soups or as a vegetable.

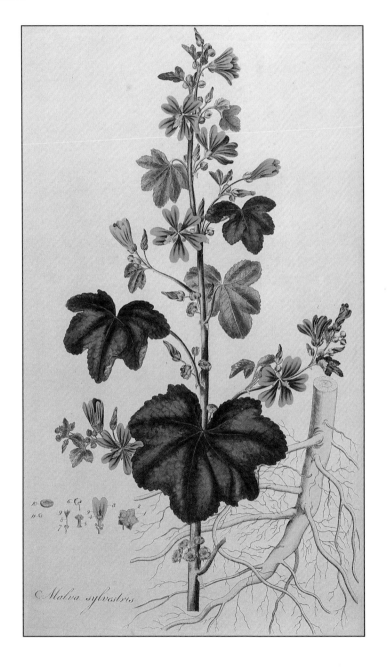

Malva sylvestris

(MALLOW FAMILY—*MALVACEAE*)

(GOOSEFOOT FAMILY—*CHENOPODIACEAE*)

MANDRAKE
Mandragora officinarum

And Reuben went in the days of the wheat harvest, and found mandrakes in the field, and brought them unto his mother Leah. Then Rachel said to Leah, Give me, I pray thee, of thy son's mandrakes. And she said unto her, Is it a small matter that thou hast taken my husband? and wouldest thou take away my son's mandrakes also? And Rachel said, Therefore he shall lie with thee to night for thy son's mandrakes.

(GENESIS 30: 14–15)

Although the mandrake does not grow in Mesopotamia where Jacob, Rachel and Leah worked through their uneasy relationships, this translation of the Hebrew *dudaim* is admirably suited to the context as the mandrake was greatly prized both as an aphrodisiac and as an inducer of fertility. The irony in this case however was that Leah who 'hired' Joseph with her son's mandrakes, conceived and bore yet another son, whereas Rachel who had been barren for many years had to wait still longer for the birth of her son Joseph.

Of course in the Bible there is little reference to the successful healing faculties of plants since this would naturally detract from acceptance of *God's* powers, so Rachel's superstitious behaviour must necessarily go unrewarded in this exclusively divine field:

Lo, children are an heritage of the LORD: and the fruit of the womb is his reward

(PSALMS 127: 3)

The Greeks valued mandrake mostly for its power 'to provoke venery', but it was also used as an anaesthetic (the patient chewed a piece of root before the operation) and to procure sleep in cases of continual pain:

. . . the rind thereof medled with wine . . . gene to them to drink that shall be cut in their body, for they should slepe and not fele the sore knitting.

(BARTHOLOMEW)

The root is actually more like that of parsley but it was often carved by the Arabs to make a crude figure, and in Europe the same was done to roots of bryony in order to deceive unsuspecting purchasers. In early herbals mandrake roots are given human form.

There were many superstitions regarding this plant, which Pythagoras first described as anthropomorphic, because of its forked root which gave it a supposed resemblance to the human form. It was believed that the plant would shriek horribly when dug up and that the hearer of such an unearthly sound could not survive. So, dogs were used to dig up the roots. By Gerard's time some scepticism was being cast upon the unearthly powers of mandrake:

There have been many ridiculous tales brought up of this plant, whether of olde wives or some runnagate surgeons or phisickmongers, I know not. . . .

(*Gerard's* HERBALL, *1597*)

However, recent research has shown that the plant does undoubtedly contain both aphrodisiac and sedative qualities—the latter, unfortunately, is in greater strength! The smell is powerful, and among westerners sometimes considered unpleasant or even fetid, which has given rise to some dispute about the reference to mandrake in SONG OF SOLOMON:

> *The* mandrakes *give a smell, and at our gates are all manner of pleasant fruits, new and old, which I have laid up for thee, O my beloved.*
>
> (SONG OF SOLOMON 7: 13)

It must be accepted however, that east and west must differ sometimes when it comes to tastes, or smells, or sounds, but Culpeper certainly refers to the practice of smelling the fruits, or *apples*, to induce sleep and it is agreed that the aroma is the heavy narcotic one of the *Solanaceous* plants—which family includes tobacco and deadly nightshade, as well as mandrake.

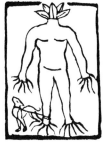

A 15TH CENTURY
WOODCUT OF
THE MANDRAKE ROOT

(POTATO FAMILY—*SOLANACEAE*)

MILLET

Panicum miliaceum
Sorghum bicolor

Take thou also unto thee wheat, and barley, and beans, and lentiles, and millet, and fitches, and put them in one vessel, and make thee bread thereof, according to the number of the days that thou shalt lie upon thy side, three hundred and ninety days shalt thou eat thereof.

(EZEKIEL 4: 9)

The Hebrew *dohan*, translated as millet above, is only once mentioned in the Bible and it is possible that either millet or similar sorghum was intended, as both were in early cultivation. The latter however is actually more suited to conditions in Israel, not requiring irrigation as millet does. Ezekiel's symbolic bread must have been coarse, but nourishing nonetheless with its mixture of pulses and grains—millet is nutritionally rich.

Such a bread would not have been leavened and would have consisted of a thin cake baked traditionally on a flat stone raised from the ground by a small stone at each corner with a fire underneath—of cow dung in Ezekiel's case.

The common people in Arabia have little other food but bad bread made of durra . . . a sort of coarse millet *by kneading it with camel's milk, oil, butter or grease. I could not eat of this bread at first, and would have preferred to it the worst bread I had ever eaten in Europe; but the people of the country, being accustomed to it, prefer it to barley-bread, which they think too light.*

(*Niebuhr's* ARABIA, *1744*)

Sorghum, also called great Indian or Italian millet, is still cultivated in the Middle East. It is extremely productive, will grow on poor soils and is used for food and for the fermentation of beer. According to Mrs Beeton (1861) it was also made into a coarse bread by the Italians and used for animal feed, while a more delicate, yellow version was made into puddings.

'Panicled' millet (*Panicum miliaceum*) is similarly productive but is only now being seriously considered in the west although it has long been an important crop in Africa, Asia and northern China. It is the staple diet of the *Hunza*, a Himalayan tribe famous for longevity, and is appearing increasingly in vegetarian cookbooks as a nutritious alternative to rice for risottos and pilaus.

. . . the nations who make use of it grind it, in the primitive manner, between two stones, and make it into a diet which cannot be properly called bread, but rather a kind of soft thin cake half-baked. When we take into account that the Arabians are fond of lizards and locusts as articles of food, their cuisine, altogether, is scarcely a tempting one.

(*Mrs Beeton*, BOOK OF HOUSEHOLD MANAGEMENT, *1861*)

More often than not to be found in budgies' cages in the West, millet also figures briefly in Gerard's HERBALL where he quotes the old Italian recipe below for quenching thirst and procuring sweat:

SIRUPUS AMBROSII

Take of unhusked Mill a sufficient quantitie, boile it till it be broken; then take five ounces of the hot decoctation, and adde thereto two ounces of the best white wine, and so give it hot unto the patient, being well covered with clothes, and then he will sweat thoroughly.

Panicum miliaceum.

(GRASS FAMILY—*GRAMINEAE*)

MINT

Mentha longifolia

But woe unto you, Pharisees! for ye tithe mint *and rue and all manner of herbs, and pass over judgment and the love of God: these ought ye to have done, and not leave the other undone.*

(LUKE 11: 42)

Mint does not appear at all in the *Old Testament*, and only twice in the *New*—above, and in the corresponding passage in MATTHEW 23: 23, as a humble tithable produce. Apparently however, the Jews were not strictly obliged by law to give the tithe (or tenth part of the crop) of such herbs as these, but only of such as could be understood as income or revenue. But the Pharisees in their hypocrisy, wishing to distinguish themselves by more scrupulous and literal observance of the law, gave tithes of these while ignoring the more important matters of justice, mercy and truth. There are several species of mint growing wild in the Holy Land and *Mentha longifolia*, or horsemint, is the most common. They grow in damp situations, by the sides of streams and ditches and the herb gets its name from a tale of Roman mythology, concerning the nymph Minthe, a daughter of the river Cocytus, with whom Pluto fell in love. Proserpine, Queen of Hell, discovered her husband's amour and changed his mistress into a moisture-loving herb. Mint was a garden plant too, in Bible lands, an important flavouring for food and of great medicinal value as well as being deliciously fresh and aromatic:

The savour or smell of the water Mint rejoyceth the hart of man, for which cause they strowe it in chambers and places of recreation, pleasure, and repose, and where feasts and banquets are made.

(Gerard's HERBALL 1597)

The Pilgrim Fathers brought mint to America and the Romans had introduced garden varieties into Britain along with other culinary herbs. Apart from using it as a flavouring for food it was made into a paste with honey, which Roman ladies used to sweeten their breath or disguise the smell of forbidden wine. Mint is still a favourite flavouring for toothpaste, mouthwashes and chewing gums and its uses in the kitchen and in the confectionery industry are endless.

Medicinally it is used mainly as an aromatic stimulant or carminative, but it is an antiseptic, expectorant, antispasmodic and tonic too. Mint tea, made by infusing 4 or 5 leaves in a cupful of boiling water is refreshing and good for headaches, nausea and digestive disorders, while inhalations using 40 or 50 grams of leaves to a litre of boiling water are recommended for chronic coughs, asthma and bronchitis. 'It stirreth up venery, or bodily lust' says Culpeper and the 17th century herbalist Parkinson relates how Aristotle and others 'forbade Mints to be used of Souldiers in the time of warre, because they thought it did so much incite to Venery, that it tooke away, or at least abated their animosity or courage to fight.'[11]

MOUTHWASH FOR BAD BREATH
(Old Italian recipe)

Add 30 grams (1 oz) of fresh mint leaves and a few drops of essence to a litre (2 pt) of good quality white wine. Leave for 48 hours then filter the wine and use several times a day to rinse the mouth.[12]

(MINT FAMILY—*LABIATAE*)

Flora Danica Tab. CCCCLXXXIV.

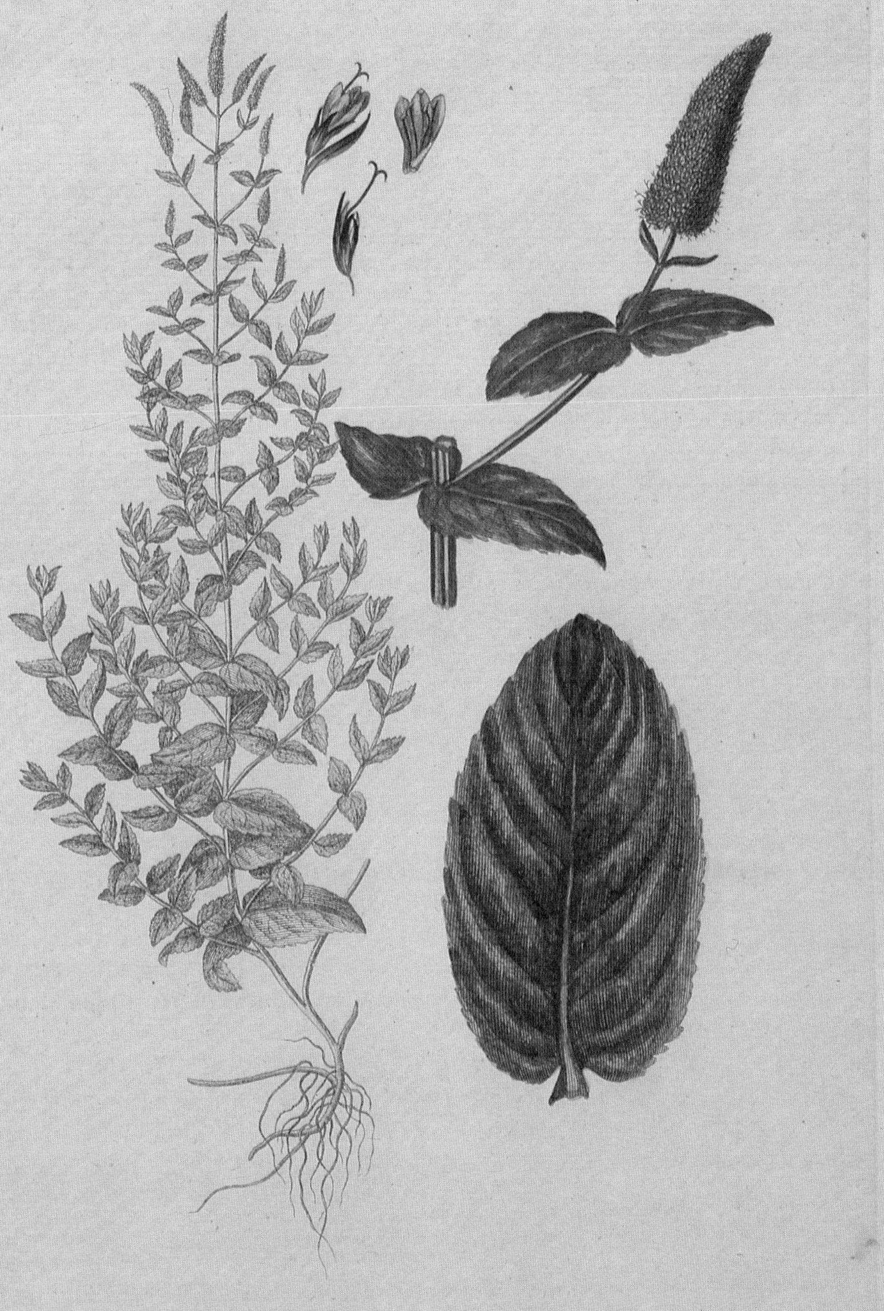

MUSTARD

Brassica nigra

The kingdom of heaven is like to a grain of mustard seed, which a man took, and sowed in his field: which indeed is the least of all seeds: but when it is grown, it is the greatest among herbs, and becometh a tree, so that the birds of the air come and lodge in the branches thereof.

(MATTHEW 13: 31–32)

Although one would not immediately think of *Brassica nigra* as a plant of tree-like proportions, in fact, in the Middle East it does fulfil all the requirements of the parable. It is a familiar plant with minute seeds, an annual which grows with extraordinary rapidity and which can reach a height of 2 metres or more. So it is conspicuously large among the herbs of the Sea of Galilee, and its seeds and branches are certainly attractive to small birds.

There are two species of mustard, black mustard (*B. nigra*) and white mustard (*Sinapis alba*). Both occur in the Holy Land but *B. nigra* is the one mentioned in the Bible. It was cultivated in biblical times, and was used both for flavouring and medicine as it is to this day, though it is most valued now as a condiment, along with white mustard.

The seede of Mustard *pound with vineger, is an excellent sauce, good to be eaten with any grosse meates either fish or flesh, bicause it doth helpe digestion, warmeth the stomacke, and provoketh appetite.*

wrote Gerard in the 16th century, and today's mustard recipes are basically the same. Most countries have their own styles and specialities however: mustard is one of the oldest condiments in French cookery and it is usually sold in the form of mustard flour mixed with wine vinegar or grape-must and flavoured with aromatic herbs and spices such as tarragon or green peppercorns—the best coming from the regions of Dijon and Bordeaux.

The Romans loved mustard; they ate it with sausages, stuffed udder and boar, and used it in their complex Apician sauces. The famous *mostarda di frutta* of Cremona is surely of ancient origin with its combination of sweet and sour flavours. Whole fruit such as plums, figs, cherries, apricots, little oranges, slices of melon and so on are preserved in a sugar syrup and flavoured with oil and mustard and garlic. This unique preserve is eaten with cold ham or tongue, turkey or pheasant and you can buy it in Italian delicatessens. English mustard is quite different. The flour is mixed with cold water and a little salt, and stirred well so that there are no lumps. Sometimes cream was used for a milder mustard, and occasionally sherry, and the preparation always completed just before it was needed. Mustard was (and still is, in France and Scandinavia) a traditional accompaniment to herring and mackerel and one early English hors d'oeuvre was brawn with a mustard sauce—served with malmsey at the enthronement of Archbishop Nevill in 1467.

I make my own mustard by grinding the white seed roughly in an electric coffee grinder, mixing it with white wine vinegar and honey, and flavouring it with salt and freshly ground pepper.

Medicinally mustard is still important, being a stimulant, diuretic and emetic and in the form of a poultice or as mustard paper (Charta Sinapis) it is employed externally as a counter-irritant. The oil which is obtained by pressure from the seeds is used instead of camphorated oil on the chest, or as a liniment for rheumatic joints, and mustard baths for the feet are recommended for sleeplessness and incipient colds. Mustard increases the flow of saliva and gastric juice and is used as an emetic to cure cases of poisoning. (Use 1 tablespoon in a tumbler of hot water.) In the 19th century this was also the common remedy in asphyxia caused by choke-damp of coal mines, and usually succeeded in rousing the patient from torpor.

(CABBAGE FAMILY—*CRUCIFERAE*)

MYRRH

Commiphora abyssinica

Now when every maid's turn was come to go in to king Ahasuerus, after that she had been twelve months, according to the manner of the women, for so were the days of their purification accomplished, to wit, six months with oil of myrrh, *and six months with sweet odours, and with other things for the purifying of the women; then thus came every maiden into the king. . . .*

(ESTHER 2: 12–13)

When King Ahasuerus decided to replace his Queen, who had humiliated him by her disobedience, he sent for the most beautiful virgins in the country, and shut them up in his harem for a year, during which time they were anointed and embellished with the costliest cosmetics before being presented to him for his choice. (Esther was the girl on whom this doubtful honour was bestowed.) Myrrh, which appears in the *New Testament* both at the birth and death of Christ, was perhaps the most expensive and precious of all the resins used in perfumery and medicine:

A bundle of myrrh *is my well-beloved unto me; he shall lie all night betwixt my breasts.*

(SONG OF SOLOMON 1: 13)

It was one of the gifts brought by the three wise men to the infant Jesus, and according to the Gospel of St Mark, was offered to him as an anodyne before the crucifixion:

. . . and they gave him to drink wine mingled with myrrh: *but he received it not . . .*

(MARK 15: 23)

and it was used with aloes to embalm his body. Myrrh was an ingredient of incense and featured importantly in the holy oil of EXODUS 30: 23 along with sweet cinnamon, sweet calamus, cassia and olive oil.

Myrrha was a daughter of Cinyras, King of Cyprus, who became enamoured of her father and introduced herself, incognita, into his bed. But when Cinyras discovered that he had committed incest, he tried to stab his daughter

and Myrrha fled through Arabia and Panchaia and wandered for nine months until she reached Sabaea where she begged for mercy and was changed into a tree which bears her name . . . and still she weeps and warm drops flow from the tree. And the child which was conceived in sin was delivered from the tree in silent agony and washed in her tears. This was Adonis, who became the darling of the Goddess Venus.

(*Ovid,* METAMORPHOSES, *Book 10*)

The *Commiphoras* are small and thorny trees which grow on arid and rocky ground in Arabia, Ethiopia and Somaliland. The latter country exports myrrh, an oleo-gum-resin which exudes naturally but is more efficiently collected by wounding the bark of the tree. It is aromatic, bitter and acrid in taste and is a tonic, astringent and stimulant. The substance occurs in the form of tears, said to be those perpetually shed by Cinyras' daughter.

The myrrh of GENESIS (43: 11): 'carry down the man a present, a little balm, and a little honey, spices, and *myrrh*, nuts and almonds . . .' was probably not the true myrrh (which almost certainly was not imported at that time) but the gum exuded by a species of rock rose, *Cistus incanus*, which is known as ladanum. It was important until quite recently not only as a perfume or incense but also medicinally. Tournefort (RELATION D'UN VOYAGE DU LEVANT, 1777) describes how it was gathered using a kind of whip to which it adhered, and Dioscorides mentions that ladanum used to be collected by goats. It would stick to their beards and the peasants would comb it out and form it into little cakes. It is a beautiful plant with lovely flowers, their petals crumpled like poppies' and of an equally ephemeral nature. Although native to Gilead and common in Spain and Portugal, rock roses grow well in moderate climates too:

> *I have sene it in Italy in certaine gardines, and ones in Englande, in my Lordes gardine at Sion.*
>
> (*Turner*, A NEW HERBALL, *1568*)

(FRANKINCENSE FAMILY—*BURSERACEAE*)

MYRTLE

Myrtus communis

Instead of the thorn shall come up the fir tree, and instead of the brier shall come up the myrtle *tree: and it shall be to the LORD for a name, for an everlasting sign that shall not be cut off.*

(ISAIAH 55: 13)

Not strictly a tree, but an evergreen shrub which can grow up to 2 metres, the myrtle has delicate white flowers and sweetish, astringent blue-black berries. It is beautiful and fragrant, and so appears among the chosen trees of ISAIAH 41: 19:

I will plant in the wilderness the cedar, the shittah tree, and the myrtle, *and the oil tree; I will set in the desert the fir tree, and the pine, and the box tree together.*

Hadas is the Hebrew word for myrtle, and *Hadassah*, the feminine form, was the original Hebrew name of Esther (ISAIAH 2: 7). The myrtle was regarded as the emblem of love and dedicated to beauty. Venus took refuge behind a myrtle bush when she was surprised at her bath by a troop of satyrs and she was crowned with myrtle after her victory over Juno and Pallas.

The myrtle-wreath was won by generals who were victorious without bloodshed, and the Romans and Sabines laid down their arms by a myrtle tree when they were reconciled. In ancient Greece the myrtle was significant in art and poetry, dedicated to Aphrodite (Greek equivalent of Venus, goddess of love) and important in betrothal rites. (Myrtle appears nowadays in bridal bouquets). Wine was made from the berries, and the Romans flavoured their food and wine with the leaves and berries—myrtles were particularly prized in sauces to accompany wild boar. In Egypt the dried leaves were powdered in a mortar, sifted and used with olive oil to anoint the bodies of infants to toughen the skin and protect against chafing. Italian ladies believed this tree of Venus to be favourable to beauty, so they used distilled myrtle water in their baths, and in modern Italy, besides being an important ornamental garden plant, a decoction of the leaves is recommended for bronchial complaints.

It is good to bathe with the decoction hereof made with wine, lims that are out of joint, and burstings that are hard to be cured, and ulcers also of the outward parts: it helpeth spreading tetters, scowreth away the dandrafe and sores of the head, maketh the haires blacke, and keepeth them from shedding; withstandeth drunkennes, if it be taken fasting . . .

writes Gerard in 1597 giving some good reasons for planting myrtle in the garden. The plant was probably introduced into Britain by Sir Walter Raleigh from Spain at the time when he discovered the preparations for the Armada, and it thrives in mild parts of Britain. It loves a warm dry soil and can be propagated by cuttings which should be taken from vigorous young shoots in July. Myrtles make a good dense hedge, the flowers are attractive to bees and the fragrant leaves may be used in pots-pourris and sweet pots. According to Pliny, the 1st century natural historian, the most odoriferous varieties are grown in Egypt.

(MYRTLE FAMILY—*MYRTACEAE*)

Myrtus communis

NETTLE

Urtica urens

ROMAN NETTLE

Urtica pilulifera

And thorns shall come up in her palaces, nettles *and brambles in the fortresses thereof: and it shall be an habitation of dragons, and a court for owls.*

(ISAIAH 34: 13)

Three Hebrew words are translated in the Bible variously as nettle, or brier as in ISAIAH 55: 13 and EZEKIEL 2: 6:

> *And thou, son of man, be not afraid of them, neither be afraid of their words, though* briers *and thorns be with thee, and thou dost dwell among scorpions . . .*

and they probably all refer to one or other of four varieties of stinging nettles which grow in Israel and which, like nettles everywhere else, flourish chiefly where man has left his rubbish.

Nettles symbolise desolation, destruction and neglect, and their stinging qualities make for admirable metaphors. There is no suggestion therefore in the Bible of their usefulness to man either for food or medicine, although they must have grown beside other plants which were gathered with a variety of herbs as food by the poor. According to Phillips in SYLVA FLORIFERA, 1823:

> *The nettle, which our peasants drive from their fields with blows and maledictions, is a crop which the Egyptians put up frequent and fervent prayers to be blessed with. Its seed affords them an oil, while the stem furnishes them with a thread, which they weave into excellent cloth.*

'They may be found, by feeling,' wrote Culpeper, 'in the darkest night,' but they lose their sting with cooking and you can use rubber gloves to pick them anyway. The young tops can be used like spinach, for soups and soufflés, are eaten raw in salads in Italy, and also make pleasant and therapeutic country wines and beers.

> *Be not nettled, my friend, at my praise of this useful weed. In Scotland, I have eaten* Nettles, *I have slept in* Nettle-sheets, *and I have dined off a* Nettle-*tablecloth.*

wrote the Scots poet Thomas Campbell (1777–1844) in his LETTERS FROM THE SOUTH lamenting that the English had no appreciation of the nettle. Actually they had, but had forgotten it. The English, like the Scots and others, had used them at one time in cheese-making and as pot-herbs. They had also taken nettles across the Atlantic to New England in the 17th century where they quickly established themselves. The cloth was said to combine fineness with strength and some said it was superior to linen.

Medicinally, nettles—seeds, roots and young leaves—have many uses. They are tonic, stimulant and depurative, and country people drink nettle tea or beer in spring to purify the blood and clear the skin. They were an old-fashioned remedy for bed-wetting too, an excellent hair and scalp tonic which is good for dandruff and a supposed cure for impotence. 'The seede of Nettle stirreth up lust,' wrote Gerard who grew both of these varieties in his physicke garden. The Roman variety, which doesn't look like a nettle, was popular in 18th-century gardens among practical jokers, who would invite the unwary to sniff the flower buds, with painful consequences.

Urtica urens.

(NETTLE FAMILY—*URTICACEAE*)

NUTS
(*Walnut*) *Juglans regia*
(*Pistachio*) *Pistacia vera*

I went down into the garden of nuts *to see the fruits of the valley, and to see whether the vine flourished, and the pomegranates budded.*

(SONG OF SOLOMON 6: 11)

And their father Israel said unto them, If it must be so now, do this; take of the best fruits in the land in your vessels, and carry down the man a present, a little balm, and a little honey, spices, and myrrh, nuts, and almonds.

(GENESIS 43: 11)

In the first extract the nuts of the enchanting garden of the bride in SONG OF SOLOMON are walnuts, and this is the only mention of them in the Bible, although the walnut was an important tree of cultivation at that time, probably introduced into Canaan from its native Persia. The timber was used, as well as the nuts and oil.

The immature fruit and bark and leaves of walnut are greatly valued by herbalists, having alterative, laxative, astringent and detergent properties, and are used to treat skin complaints such as eczema and herpes. (Add 50 g dried bark, or a little more of fresh leaves, to a litre of boiling water; stand for several hours, strain and take a wine-glassful three times a day, using the infusion externally at the same time.) A decoction of walnut leaves is excellent as a footbath for tired and swollen feet, for chilblains, internally for fevers, and as a mouth-wash or gargle.

In the kitchen, the oil makes an interesting and unusual salad dressing for chicory, endive, radicchio or spinach. It is expensive, but has a delicious and distinctive flavour. The nuts are mixed with chopped apples, celery and mayonnaise to make the delicious American Waldorf salad.

Walnuts can be used green, before the shell hardens, for pickles, ketchups or for delicious and therapeutic liqueurs such as the French *brou de noix* which uses crushed, green walnuts and *eau-de-vie* flavoured with cinnamon, mint and cloves. These immature nuts were a popular sweetmeat in Gerard's day:

The greene and tender nuts *boyled in sugar and eaten as Suckade, are a most pleasant and delectable meate, comfort the stomacke, and expell poyson.*

(Gerard's HERBALL, 1597)

The Italians are fond of green walnuts too, and here is a traditional recipe for a liqueur which is an excellent digestif:

WALNUT LIQUEUR

500 g (1 lb) soft green walnuts
500 g (1 pt) alcohol (60 per cent)
500 g (1 pt) water
4 g ($\frac{1}{4}$ oz) cinnamon bark
20 g (1 oz) red rose petals, dried in the shade
10 g ($\frac{1}{2}$ oz) fennel seeds
4 cloves

*Put the nuts, alcohol and water in a glass container, seal and leave for 45
days. Add all the other ingredients and leave the liqueur in a dark place for
a few days. Filter and bottle.*[13]

In the passage in GENESIS, the nuts which are to represent the 'best fruits of the land'
are pistachios, prized then, as now, for their wonderful flavour. This tree, too, was
probably introduced into Israel from Persia. The nuts, which are readily available now,
though expensive, are eaten as a snack with the aperitif, or used to flavour fine pâtés and
terrines, or traditionally for ice creams, desserts and sweetmeats.

(WALNUT FAMILY—*JUGLANDACEAE*)

(CASHEW FAMILY—*ANACARDIACEAE*)

OAK

Quercus

They sacrifice upon the tops of the mountains, and burn incense upon the hills, under oaks *and poplars and elms, because the shadow thereof is good:*

(HOSEA 4: 13)

But Deborah, Rebekah's nurse died, and she was buried beneath Bethel under an oak: *and the name of it was called Allon-bachuth.*

(GENESIS 35: 8)

Not surprisingly, for a tree of such size and strength, the oak crops up frequently in the Scriptures. The Hebrew is *allon* (and *elon*, while *elah* is terebinth and this similarity has caused confusion and argument among scholars in the past). There are other similarities too. They are both majestic trees of impressive age and stature which have been revered since ancient times, and have many associations of ritual and religious practice. There are many varieties throughout the northern hemisphere, and the deciduous *Quercus ithaburensis* (Tabor Oak) and the evergreen *Quercus coccifera* (kermes oak) which are natives of the Holy Land are of suitably impressive stature to fit the contexts. Deborah's burial place was one which was reserved for the most honoured dead, and Herrick's poem of the 17th century echoes this in a rural English setting.

> *Dearest, bury me*
> *Under that holy oke; or Gospel Tree,*
> *Where, though thou see'st not, thou may'st think upon*
> *me, when you yearly go'st Procession.*

> *'To Anthea'*

Gospel trees were used for prayer, blessing, and as resting places during 'beating of the parish bounds' ceremonies—a kind of primitive marking-out of territory which took place once a year and which involved clergy and parishioners in procession. The Druids used oaks as well in their pagan rituals, whilst the Greeks held it sacred and the Romans dedicated it to Jupiter.

'The timber thereof being the glory and safety of this nation by sea,' wrote Culpeper, and it was the use of the timber in ship-building, house-building (and of the charcoal for iron-smelting, which ironically supplanted oak) which caused the British forests to dwindle so sadly. The timber is not in great demand in these days of fibre-glass, steel and concrete but it was greatly valued for its durability, hardness and elasticity, especially in ship-building. (Philip of Spain ordered the Armada to destroy the famous Forest of Dean which provided so much for the defence of Britain.) If oak has lost a good deal of its former glory it is still greatly appreciated in herbal medicine. The powdered bark of the young branches is mostly used—and this should be dried in the sun or in an airy place, and reduced to a powder using a pestle and mortar. A pinch of this will stop a nose-bleed, and an infusion is good for bathing chilblains, and for sweaty feet and armpits.

Apart from making a country wine from the leaves, a pleasant cure for bleeding or out-of-condition gums can be prepared by macerating 20 g oak leaves and 10 g medicinal hydrochloric acid in a litre of good red wine. Strain after a week and take a glass with meals.

Acorn coffee is not as bad as it sounds (it was imposed upon the Germans during the First World War) and is made by roasting the acorns in a moderate oven till dark brown and completely dry, then grinding them in a coffee grinder.

A peck of acorns a day, with a little bran, will make an hog ('tis said) increase a pound weight per diem *for two months together. They give them [acorns] also to oxen mingled with bran, chop'd or broken; otherwise they are apt to sprout and grow in their bellies.*

(John Evelyn: SYLVA)

(BEECH FAMILY—*FAGACEAE*)

OLIVE

Olea europaea

And the dove came in to him in the evening; and, lo, in her mouth was an olive leaf pluckt off: so Noah knew that the waters were abated from off the earth.

(GENESIS 8: 11)

The olive has ever since been a symbol of hope, new life, peace and reconciliation. In ancient Greece it symbolised wisdom and it was also venerated by the Romans. An olive branch was traditionally used as a peace offering and so it remains today featured on the flag of the United Nations. Olive trees grow slowly but attain a great age and there are olives in Italy said to be more than 2,000 years old. These ancient trees sprout new shoots from the gnarled old parent trunks and the psalmist refers to this when writing of the blessings of many children:

Thy wife shall be as a fruitful vine by the sides of thine house: thy children like olive plants round about thy table.

(PSALM 128: 3)

The tree, its groves, its fruit and its oil are frequently referred to in the Scriptures in poetic imagery, allegory and symbolism. Olives are a common sight in the Holy Land and many ancient stone presses still exist—even where there are no longer olive groves— testifying to their importance. The tree and its fruit touched upon almost every aspect of daily life, being used for food, fuel, light, carpentry, medicines and ointments. Medicinally, the olive is significant. Arabs say that you should take olive oil internally, externally, eternally to enjoy a long healthy life, but the leaves, bark and fruit also have their uses and a decoction of the leaves is taken for hypertension. They are astringent and antiseptic, and a similar decoction, or of the bark, is effective in cases of fever. An Italian mixture called *Balsamo del Samaritano* is used to dress wounds and soothe sunburn: Mix the following in equal parts—olive oil, white wine, egg white. Beat a little to emulsify the mixture. The oil is nutritious, demulcent and mildly laxative, and externally it is useful in cases of eczema and psoriasis. It is used in pharmacy for liniments and ointments, but can be used simply to massage the skin or as a hair conditioner.

In the kitchen it is wonderful for cooking and for salads and you can flavour it for this purpose with herbs or garlic. The finest is obtained from the first cold pressing and this is the beautiful greenish Virgin oil. Italy, Greece, Spain, Portugal and Provençe all export olives and oil but the most famous is from the province of Lucca in Tuscany. Queen Victoria's chef Francatelli recommend olives from Lucca 'being perfectly sweet, and free from any strong flavour, they are served for dessert in glasses, with a little of their own liquor in which they are served.'

We eat olives as an aperitif these days, and in the right circumstances—sun, bread, wine, they can be princely fare.

> *The simple olives, best allies of wine,*
> *Must I pass over in my bill of fare?*
> *I must, although a favourite 'plat' of mine,*
> *In Spain, and Lucca, Athens, everywhere:*
> *On them and bread 'twas oft my luck to dine,*
> *The grass my table-cloth, in open air....*

(Byron: DON JUAN Canto XV)

To prevent intoxication: If you cannot tolerate alcohol (and insist on taking it.) take a spoonful of olive oil beforehand. It will line the walls of the stomach so the alcohol will take much longer to pass through the bloodstream and will have time to be broken down by the liver.

(OLIVE FAMILY—*OLEACEAE*)

ONION

Allium cepa

We remember the fish, which we did eat in Egypt freely; the cucumbers, and the melons, and the leeks, and the onions, and the garlick.

(NUMBERS 11: 5)

This is the only mention in the Bible of these indispensable members of the lily family, for which the Israelites longed in the wilderness—curious, really, as they were all important cultivated vegetables at the time. Onions were known in Egypt more than 3,000 years before the birth of Christ, as food and for their therapeutic qualities, especially for bladder and kidney problems, and along with garlic they were important daily rations for the labourers who constructed the Pyramids. At one time, according to Pliny and Juvenal, they were objects of superstition in Egypt and Mrs Beeton refers to this too:

Like the cabbage, this plant was erected into an object of worship by the idolatrous Egyptians 2,000 years before the Christian era. . . .
(BOOK OF HOUSEHOLD MANAGEMENT, 1861)

Egyptian onions are considered sweeter and more delicious than any others and are often eaten raw with bread. They are supposed not to make the breath smell as offensively as other varieties, but this has always been a problem, and the most devoted onion-eaters are obliged to desist sometimes:

And, most dear actors, eat no onions nor garlic, for we are to utter sweet breath.
(Bottom, in Shakespeare's A MIDSUMMER NIGHT'S DREAM, Act IV, scene II)

It is a pity about the lingering aroma on the breath, because the virtues of onions are manifold, and you are advised to eat them raw as much as possible, because cooking partially destroys their active principles. Onions are tonic, diuretic, emollient and antiseptic—reputedly aphrodisiac too, hence the practice on the Continent of giving onion soup to young couples on their wedding night.

'It has been held by divers country people a great preservative against infection, to eat onions fasting, with bread and salt,' writes Culpeper in the 17th century, and the Bulgarians, who are great onion-eaters as well as yoghurt-eaters, attribute their longevity to one or other of these foods. The juice made into a syrup with honey is good for coughs and colds and asthmatic complaints, and gin in which onions have been macerated is given to cure gravel and dropsy. Preparations with onions are found in health shops in capsules and syrups, so that you can enjoy the benefits without having to resort to chewing parsley afterwards.

In the kitchen, onions are a wonderful, you might say essential, flavouring and they are incredibly versatile. It is hard to think of any country where the onion does not figure importantly—in the *haute cuisine* of France, one or other of the family (which includes the shallot) is a vital seasoning for countless classic dishes. Onions can be steamed, boiled, baked, sautéd or deep fried in batter. In the Middle East they are threaded between

112

pieces of meat on skewers and grilled over charcoal. They make wonderful soups, sauces, tarts and savoury breads, and I offer the following recipe for the simple classic French onion soup for its aphrodisiac qualities! The secret is to cook the onions very slowly at first.

FRENCH ONION SOUP

50 g (2 oz) butter
450 g (1 lb) onions, peeled and finely sliced
1 tsp sugar
2 tsp flour
1–2 litres (2–3 pt) beef stock

Melt the butter, add the onions and cook for 20–30 minutes over a low heat, stirring from time to time. Stir in the flour and cook for a minute or two. Add the stock gradually, season to taste and simmer for 15 minutes.

Before serving, you can, if you like, add a slice of toasted French bread to each bowl, sprinkle some grated gruyère cheese on top and toast under the grill.

(LILY FAMILY—*LILIACEAE*)

PALM

Phoenix dactylifera

The righteous shall flourish like the palm *tree: he shall grow like a cedar in Lebanon. Those that be planted in the house of the LORD shall flourish in the courts of our God. They shall still bring forth fruit in old age; they shall be fat and flourishing.*

(PSALM 92: 12–14)

In the Bible, where it is frequently mentioned, the date palm signifies grace, holiness, nobility and fecundity as in the psalm above. In SONG OF SOLOMON (7: 7–8) the bride is compared to a palm tree:

> *This thy stature is like to a* palm *tree, and thy breasts to clusters of grapes. I said, I will go up to the* palm *tree, I will take hold of the boughs thereof: now also thy breasts shall be as clusters of the vine, and the smell of thy nose like apples.*

It was also, along with goodly trees (possibly citrons), thick trees and willows, one of the four species mentioned in LEVITICUS 23: 40, for the Feast of Tabernacles. Palms were greatly valued and revered by the Israelites and the tree became a symbol of Judea. They appear in carvings and sculptures in architecture and King Solomon's temple had pilasters in the form of palm trees. Palms are tall and stately, growing to between 10 and 20 metres in height and they sway gracefully in the wind, seldom breaking even in the fiercest gales. The fronds were used in triumphal processions—as when Jesus entered Jerusalem on that first 'palm Sunday'.

All parts of the tree are put to ingenious use. Baskets, couches, mats and brushes are made from the leaves, garden fences and poultry cages from the branches, thread and ropes from the fibres of the boughs. The body serves for fuel and the sap provides a type of honey which can be fermented, and distilled to produce a spirit rather like aquavit. Sometimes the fruit was boiled up to make a type of honey or syrup, and this could be fermented too. It must have been similar to *arrak* (the word is from the Arabic, meaning strong liquor), which was a popular drink in Britain in the 17th and 18th centuries. Imported via the East India trade, it was distilled from rice, sugar and dates with added spices. Curiously, the date itself is not specifically mentioned in the Bible, although it was such an important foodstuff and was used medicinally too. Dates, along with figs, raisins and jujubes, are considered pectoral fruit, and these four are combined in modern herbal medicine to make a syrup for bronchitis and catarrh.

Dates have been exported worldwide for centuries. They were used in the sweet/savoury Lenten pies of the rich in medieval Europe and given with other imported dried fruits and sweetmeats as bribes for children in the nursery or treats for pregnant women. When buying dried dates, avoid the hard-packed ones and take Mrs Beeton's advice:

> *They should be large, softish, not much wrinkled, of a reddish-yellow colour outside, with a whitish membrane between the fruit and the stone.*

114

Dates are still mostly enjoyed as festive titbits, sometimes combined with almonds or marzipan, and they make a rich and nourishing addition to muesli and granola mixtures, cakes and teabreads. They don't often appear in savoury dishes as they did in the time of Apicius, the famous Roman glutton, though I'd like to experiment with his date-based sauces for venison. Gerard (1597) had mixed feelings about dates but recommended them for 'the wambling of womens stomacks that are with childe.' It is now known that dates, like figs, contain vitamins B6 (also B3, folic acid and magnesium) which are particularly needed by pregnant women and those who drink alcohol regularly. Which just goes to show that the herbalists of old can often be depended on for the sound advice that has been gleaned from centuries of experience.

(PALM FAMILY—*PALMAE*)

PINE

(Aleppo pine) *Pinus halepensis*
(Stone pine) *Pinus pinea*

It is hardly surprising that there are difficulties in identifying the various conifers mentioned in the Bible: there was little interest in botany in those days, the trees are very similar and the various timbers were utilised in much the same ways. Only the cedar of Lebanon stands apart, clearly identified in its majesty, and scholars have been arguing about the others for centuries. The Aleppo pine however is known to have been widespread in the Holy Land, and this is probably the tree referred to in NEHEMIAH (8: 15):

> . . . *Go forth unto the mount, and fetch olive branches, and* pine *branches, and myrtle branches, and palm branches, and branches of thick trees, to make booths, as it is written.*

Stone pines grew there too, and this is most likely the tree in ISAIAH 44: 14, translated as cypress in the King James version and holm tree in some others (this latter never grew in the Holy Land). *Pinus pinea* is the distinctive umbrella or stone pine which characterises much of the Italian landscape and whose seeds (pine nuts, or *pinoli*) are combined with basil, olive oil and parmesan cheese to make that glorious Genoese sauce—*pesto*—which is served with pasta in Italy. The delicious, delicately-flavoured little nuts are used there too in meat and game dishes, cheesecakes, festive breads, biscuits and black puddings. They are plentiful in Greece as well and are added to savoury stuffings for vine leaves (*dolmades*) and to sweet halvas and cakes.

The various pines (there are at least 90) have always had considerable commercial value. They tend to have straight and unbranched trunks and the wood is strong and versatile. Moreover the resin is distilled to produce oil of turpentine which is used medicinally in kidney and bladder complaints—formulae discovered on Egyptian papyri of the time of the Pharaohs show that turpentine and pitch were prescribed by doctors then too, and Hippocrates recommended it for pneumonia.

> *The liquid Rosins are very fitly mixed in ointments, commended for the healing up of greene wounds . . . there is gathered out from the Rosins as from Frankencense, a congealed smoke, [a type of kohl] . . . which serveth for medicines that beautifie the eie lids, and cure the fretting sores of the corners of the eies, and also watering eies. . . .*
>
> (*Gerard's* HERBALL, 1597)

The green cones and needles are the parts generally used today. Boiled up in water, strained and the liquid added to the bath, they soothe rheumatic pains and help skin diseases such as eczema. Such a bath is wonderfully aromatic and refreshing too. You can use pine needle in pot-pourri, or sweet bags or in herb pillows, and the essence can be used to scent home-made candles.

Here is the famous Genoese sauce, which, if made in larger quantities, can be stored in jars covered with a layer of olive oil.

PESTO
1 large bunch of fresh basil
2–3 cloves garlic
25 g (1 oz) grated parmesan cheese
25 g (1 oz) pine nuts
50 g (2 oz) olive oil

Pound the basil in a mortar with the garlic, pine nuts and a little salt, then add the oil a little at a time, stirring steadily, as if making mayonnaise. Serve with any pasta.

Pinus halepensis MILL.

(PINE FAMILY—*PINACEAE*)

117

POMEGRANATE

Punica granatum

And they came unto the brook of Eshcol, and cut down from thence a branch with one cluster of grapes, and they bare it between two upon a staff; and they brought of the pomegranates, *and of the figs.*

(NUMBERS 13: 23)

The pomegranate occupies a special place in the Bible. Not only is it one of the choice fruits brought back by Moses' spies from Canaan as evidence of the fecundity of the Promised Land, but it features in the poetic imagery of the SONG OF SOLOMON where the bride's beauty is likened to the fruit:

Thy temples are like a piece of a pomegranate *within thy locks.* . . .

(4: 3)

Thy plants are an orchard of pomegranates, *with pleasant fruits.* . . .

(4: 13)

The pomegranate with its many seeds and delicious red juice was a symbol of fertility, and its beautifully shaped fruit with a crown-like calyx appeared in sculptures and embroideries, on furniture and carved columns and on the hems of the robes of high priests.

And beneath upon the hem of it thou shalt make pomegranates *of blue, and of purple, and of scarlet, round about the hem thereof; and bells of gold between them round about: A golden bell and a* pomegranate, *a golden bell and a* pomegranate, *upon the hem of the robe round about.*

(EXODUS 28: 33–34)

The pomegranate is a small tree, not more than 5 metres high with round rosy fruit the size of apples and very beautiful red flowers which on account of their beauty and fragrance symbolised the loveliness of the coming of spring. It is of Asian origin but thrives throughout the Mediterranean and is often grown in parks and gardens for its ornamental value. All parts of the tree—flowers, fruit, root, bark—were of medicinal importance and the rind of the fruit and the root bark appear in the BRITISH PHARMACEUTICAL CODEX. Powerfully astringent, they are used in the treatment of diarrhoea and tapeworm, and you can prepare a mouth-wash with the flowers for gingivitis or sore throats. Make an infusion with 25 g flowers to half a litre of boiling water and use this mouthwash several times a day, or as a gargle in the case of sore throats.

In Culpeper's day (mid-17th century) you could buy the flowers in powdered form 'under the title of *balustines*', and the syrup made of the fruit, according to Gerard, was 'profitable against the longing of women with childe.' The juice and the seeds are widely used in cookery by the Persians who enjoy sweet/sour dishes such as *Faisinjan*, which is a classic Persian stew made with duck, ground walnuts and pomegranate syrup. Often too the seeds are flavoured with rosewater and eaten as a dessert or a cooling drink prepared from them. Grenadine is a syrup of pomegranate which is popular in France, especially with children, but it also features in many cocktail recipes:

HARRY'S PICK-ME-UP (1927)
1 teaspoonful of Grenadine syrup
1 glass of Brandy
Juice of ½ a lemon

Shake well and strain into medium sized wine glass, and fill balance with Champagne.[14]

Wine of pomegranate is mentioned in SONG OF SOLOMON:

... I would cause thee to drink of spiced wine of the juice of the pomegranate.

(8: 2)

and this could mean either a wine fermented from the juice, as was sometimes made in Persia, or grape wine acidulated with pomegranate. It sounds seductive enough!

Punica Granatum

(POMEGRANATE FAMILY—*PUNICACEAE*)

119

POPLAR

Populus alba

STORAX

Styrax officinalis

And Jacob took him rods of green poplar, *and of the hazel and chestnut tree; and pilled white strakes in them, and made the white appear which was in the rods. And he set the rods which he had pilled before the flocks in the gutters in the watering troughs when the flocks came to drink, that they should conceive when they came to drink. And the flocks conceived before the rods, and brought forth cattle ringstraked, speckled, and spotted.*

(GENESIS 30: 37–39)

When Jacob decided at last to take his uneasy ménage à trois back to his homeland, wives Leah and Rachel plus their assorted offspring which included those of slave-girls Bilhah and Zilpah, he asked his father-in-law Laban, as wages for many years of faithful service, that he might remove any black and brindled lambs and spotted goats from Laban's flocks. A fair deal, one might say, but Laban removed all such animals that very night and gave them to his sons, so Jacob had to resort to 'magic' for justice, as above, and this resulted in vigorous and numerous flocks of his own. ('Jacob sheep', which enlightened landowners these days stock on their estates for aesthetic effect, remind us of the story.)

White poplar gets its name both from its bark and the white underside of its leaves, and it was prized for its soft, easily-worked wood, which was perfect for many small domestic and agricultural tools. Poplar wood is light and so has been used over the centuries to make boxes and packing cases to cut down on carriage costs. Nails do not split the wood easily either, but it makes a poor fuel, roasting rather than burning, and giving off a good deal of smoke and no flame—which fact could recommend it for building purposes!

In Italy, it is the tall, tapering Lombardy poplar which characterises the landscape. It is planted sometimes to support the vine and its timber is used to make the crates which transport the grapes.

Poplars, which prefer to grow by riverbanks, are best planted in moist ground and will effectively drain it and manure the soil with their leaves, so as to make it fit for meadow or pasture.

The black poplar (*Populus nigra*) is the variety which is most valued medicinally for its astringent buds, but the bark of *Populus alba* is used to this day in the Middle East and in Europe for its tonic and febrifuge properties. The leaves were considered an infallible cure for gout, and the buds of both black and white 'have an agreeable perfume in springtime and when pressed between the fingers yield a balsamic resinous substance, which when extracted by spirits of wine smells like *storax*' (Phillips SYLVA FLORIFERA, 1823). This could explain the misunderstandings which arise from the Hebrew word for poplar (*livneh*) being homonymous with that used for *Styrax officinalis*, which is the plant referred to in HOSEA 4: 13:

They sacrifice upon the tops of the mountains, and burn incense upon the hills, under oaks and poplars *and elms, because the shadow thereof is good. . . .*

It is the coupling with oaks and terebinths ('elms') in this passage which makes the identification of *Styrax* definite, as they have grown side by side since biblical days. The Euphrates poplar, *Populus euphratica* could well have been the tree wrongly identified as mulberry in 2 SAMUEL 5: 23–24, on account of the rustling sound its leaves make in the wind.

The White Poplar Tree.

Publish'd Jan.ʸ 1ˢᵗ 1776, by A. Hunter, M.D. as the Act directs.

J. Miller del. & Sc.

P. 208.

(WILLOW FAMILY—*SALICACEAE*)

ROSE

Rosa canina, Rosa phoenicia

The wilderness and the solitary place shall be glad for them; and the desert shall rejoice, and blossom as the rose.

(ISAIAH 35: 1)

Although rose in this case and in SONG OF SOLOMON 2: 1 ('I am the rose of Sharon, a lily of the valleys') should properly be translated lily, and the true rose is not actually named in the *Authorised Version* of the Bible, it was almost certainly one of the flowers of the field of the *Old Testament* and one of Christ's lilies of the field in the *New*.

There are several species of native roses in Israel, *Rosa canina* which is common in many parts of temperate Eurasia and northern Africa, and *Rosa phoenicia* which is confined to the eastern Mediterranean being the commonest. Roses, however, were cultivated in Bible times for their scent, their beauty and for their various domestic and cosmetic purposes.

The Rose doth deserve the chiefest and most principall place among all flowers whatsoever . . . for his beautie, vertues, and his fragrant and odoriferous smell; . . .

wrote Gerard in 1597. Roses were distilled then in vast quantities to make rosewater for flavouring, perfumes and herbal remedies.

The distilled water of Roses is good for the strengthening of the hart, and refreshing of the spirits. . . . The same being put in junketting dishes, cakes, sawces, and many other pleasant things, giveth a fine and delectable taste.

(*Gerard's* HERBALL, *1597*)

Rosewater is still used in Middle-Eastern cookery, in jams, sweetmeats, syrups and conserves, while perfumes there are probably as popular today as they were in Bible times. Damascus is noted for the distilling of rosewater, and that valuable essential oil, *Otto* (or attar) *of Roses*, is obtained by distillation of the damask rose—*Rosa damascena*. These roses are cultivated in Bulgaria, as well as in Damascus, and the oil is mainly used in perfumery, for lozenges, dentifrices and toilet preparations. You can buy oil of roses in good herbalists to make pots-pourris and sweetbags, or to scent home-made candles and soaps. Rosewater is available in most chemists and I use it to flavour Turkish delight, fruit salads, and compôtes, as well as using it as a delightful and inexpensive face lotion.

Rosa canina.

The traditional 'Rose of Jericho' is something quite different, and has not the slightest resemblance to a true rose. It is a low, annual crucifer, *Anastatica hierochuntica*, which after maturing dries up, its branches curve inwards and it forms a round fibrous ball. When placed in water, it absorbs moisture, the branches expand and it opens up again. It is a rather unattractive curiosity.

(ROSE FAMILY—*ROSACEAE*)

RUE

Ruta chalepensis, Ruta graveolens

But woe unto you, Pharisees! for ye tithe mint and rue and all manner of herbs, and pass over judgment and the love of God: these ought ye to have done, and not to leave the other undone.

(LUKE 11: 42)

This is the only reference to rue in the Bible, and because it is such an acrid and bitter herb, it is most likely that it was cultivated for its medicinal properties rather than for flavouring food. The Greeks and Romans valued rue—particularly Hippocrates— and it was important in the Middle Ages as a protection against plague.

The leaves of Rue eaten with the kernels of Walnuts, or figs stamped togither and made into a masse or paaste, is good against all evil aires, the pestilence or plague

wrote Gerard in 1597, and rue had always been considered a powerful repellent of all kinds of vermin—moths, mice, fleas and other insects. Early American colonial recipes for the herbal vinegars that were used to disinfect sickrooms and ward off germs, contain rue, and the herb was hung in wardrobes and placed in linen chests as well.

Shakespeare, who had an intimate knowledge of herbs, knew it well:

There's rosemary, that's for remembrance; pray you, love, remember; and there is pansies, that's for thoughts. There's fennel for you, and columbines: there's rue for you; and here's some for me; we may call it a herb of grace o' Sundays; O, you must wear your rue with a difference. There's a daisy; I would give you some violets but they withered all when my father died.

(HAMLET, *Act IV*, scene 5)

This was Ophelia, after the killing of her father, and her little bouquet of herbs contained a message as bitter as the bitterest rue. Fennel was for dissembling, columbine for unchastity, daisy for faithlessness, rue for repentance, contrition and grief. It was called the herb of grace or repentance because holy water used to be sprinkled at High Mass using 'brushes' of rue.

The plant is stimulating and antispasmodic and is still sometimes employed in infusions as an emmenagogue. In Italy today an eye wash is prepared by boiling 100 g of leaves in half a litre of water. This is strained after 15 minutes and used to bathe tired and red eyes and to clear the sight. A leaf or two of rue, chewed, is effective in relieving nervous headaches, giddiness and palpitations. Perhaps you can experience similar benefits by imbibing one variety of Italian grappa which contains the herb.

Rue is a pretty plant, a hardy evergreen shrub with yellow flowers and blue-green leaves which looks well in a herbaceous border. *Ruta graveolens* is the variety most commonly found in Europe and North America, but *Ruta chalepensis*, or Aleppo rue, was probably the rue of the Bible.

(RUE FAMILY—*RUTACEAE*)

126

SAFFRON

Crocus sativus

Thy plants are an orchard of pomegranates, with pleasant fruits; camphire, with Spikenard and saffron; *calamus and cinnamon, with all trees of frankincense; myrrh and aloes, with all the chief spices.*

(SONG OF SOLOMON 4: 13–14)

This is the only mention of saffron in the Bible, where it is in company with cultivated aromatics and with the costliest of imported items of luxury and sensuality. Saffron is a beautiful and delicate autumn flowering crocus and it was once used medicinally as well as for colouring and flavouring food. 'It possesses considerable power as an exitant,' wrote Graves in HORTUS MEDICUS of 1834, and in small doses it is tonic and stimulant, whereas in larger ones it is antispasmodic and sedative. In overdose it produces all the symptoms of intoxication and when taken habitually it colours the perspiration, urine and saliva yellow, and imparts to them its distinctive odour.

The parts of the plant used are the dried stigmas, so saffron has always been an expensive commodity because of the labour involved in gathering it. It is estimated that in order to obtain one ounce of saffron, well over 4,000 flowers are required! It was a very popular seasoning in medieval times for those who could afford it (saffron cost 14 or 15 shillings a pound in the 13th and 14th centuries in Britain). Spain exported it, and Italy too, though to a lesser degree. It was grown in England too, hence place-names such as Saffron Walden and Saffron Hill.

It was used to flavour and colour the medieval fish jellies of Europe, and for colouring cheese before it was discovered that marigold petals were cheaper and almost as effective. Saffron was even used to flavour such unlikely vegetables as leeks, cabbages, rapes and parsnips, but in Britain it is now out of favour except in old-fashioned cakes and tea-breads such as Cornish saffron cake.

In Europe saffron is a classic ingredient of fish soups (e.g. *bouillabaisse* of the South of France) and rice dishes such as Milanese risotto and popular liqueurs like the Livornese *strega* or the French *chartreuse*.

In the Middle East it is a popular spice and in Morocco and Persia it is used extensively in all sorts of dishes for its colour and distinctive aroma. Saffron is still expensive, and because it can easily be adulterated in powdered form, it is wisest to buy it in 'threads' or stigmas.

Culpeper recommends saffron as an 'elegant and useful aromatic, of a strong penetrating smell, and a warm, pungent, bitterish taste,' but warns that its use 'ought to be moderate and seasonable; for when the dose is too large, it produces a heaviness of the head, and a sleepiness; some have fallen into an immoderate convulsive laughter, which ended in death.' But considering the current price of saffron there is little need to worry about health hazards from overdose.

CHARTREUSE
1 litre alcohol (70 per cent)
saffron
1·5 g angelica root
0·5 g fennel seeds
2 g aniseed
750 g sugar
1·5 litres water

Put the alcohol in a dark bottle. Add the fennel seed, a pinch of saffron, the angelica root and the aniseed. Shake well and leave to infuse for two days. Make a thick syrup with the sugar and water and mix with the infusion. Allow to cool then filter and pour into dark bottles. Close tightly and leave in a cool place for a few months before drinking.

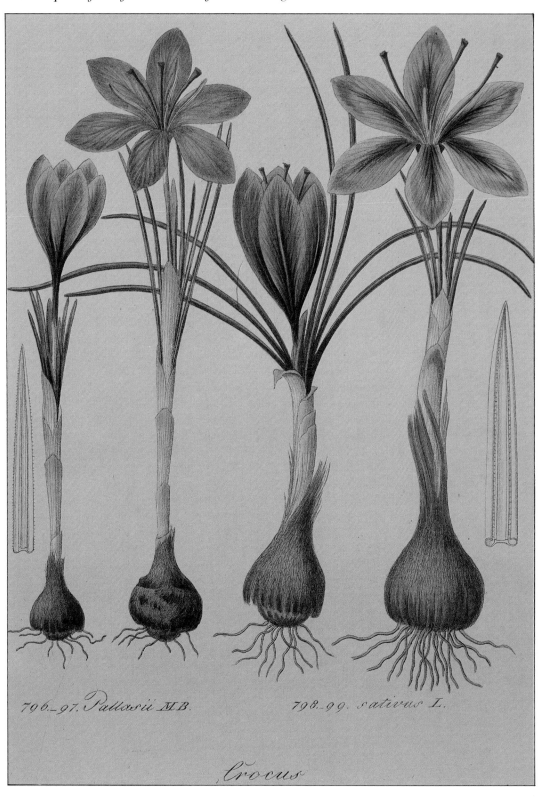

796.–97. *Pallasii* M.B.   798.–99. *sativus* L.

Crocus

(IRIS FAMILY—*IRIDACEAE*)

129

SHITTAH

Acacia raddiana

And they shall make an ark of shittim *wood . . . And thou shalt overlay it with pure gold, within and without shalt thou overlay it, and shalt make upon it a crown of gold round about.*

(EXODUS 25: 10–11)

The tabernacle, or meeting tent, and the altar were also constructed of this wood by the Israelites in Sinai. It is the common acacia and is the only timber tree of any size in that desert, with a tough, smooth and beautiful wood. Its main flowering season is in March/April, but it flowers again in December and the twisted pods which contain the fruits are eaten by animals. The prophet Isaiah mentions it along with other fragrant trees:

I will plant in the wilderness the cedar, the shittah *tree, and the myrtle, and the oil tree; I will set in the desert the fir tree, and the pine, and the box tree together: That they may see, and know, and consider, and understand together, that the hand of the LORD hath done this, and the Holy One of Israel hath created it.*

(ISAIAH 41: 19–20)

Here is a curious metaphor illustrative of the mysteries and difficulties in identifying the plants of the Bible. Why group the acacia with the trees of cultivation and civilization, and why suggest planting it in the desert when it is already abundant there?

There are many species of acacia throughout the world and Gerard in his HERBALL of 1597 refers to the shrubby Egyptian thorn as the true one. (In addition to *Acacia raddiana*, *Acacia tortilis*, which is especially conspicuous on Mount Sinai and *Acacia seyal* are the two most common varieties.) Several of them exude gum from the stem in the form of oval or round 'tears' and this substance—gum acacia—is used in medicine as a demulcent (the best is collected in upper Egypt). Acacia gum is highly nutritious and a valuable source of food in the desert. In the western world it is used in cough mixtures and pastilles and is very soothing in inflammations of the respiratory tract.

Acacia honey is soothing too, light and delicate and slow to granulate, but this comes from the false acacia, or locust tree—*Robinia pseudoacacia*—which was introduced into Britain from North America in 1640. It is a popular ornamental tree with a hard, close-grained timber which the first British settlers used to build their houses in Boston.

The finest *Robinias* are grown from seed, though the tree is also propagated by suckers and cuttings. Sow the seed in light earth at the end of March and in about six weeks the young plants will appear: they can be transplanted the following year.

Use acacia honey to sweeten herbal teas, muesli, cakes and breads or in this pleasant dressing for fruit.

YOGHURT AND ACACIA HONEY DRESSING FOR FRUIT SALADS
1 cup yoghurt
2 tbsp acacia honey
½ tsp lemon juice
1 tbsp pineapple juice
1 tsp lemon rind (grated)
small pinch salt

Beat the yoghurt until frothy: mix well and serve with fresh fruit salad.[15]

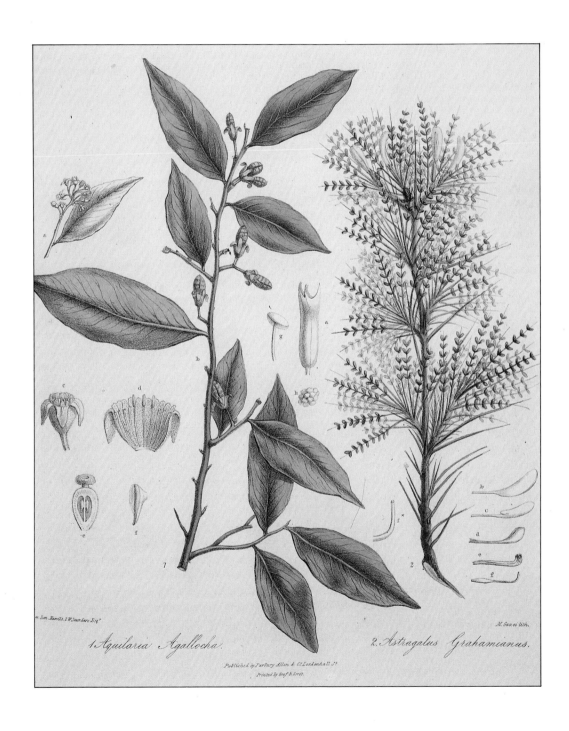

1 *Aquilaria Agallocha.*   2 *Astragalus Grahamianus.*

(PEA FAMILY—*LEGUMINOSAE*)

SPIKENARD

Nardostachys jatamansi

And every human heart that breaks
In prison cell or yard,
Is as that broken box that gave
Its treasure to the Lord
And filled the unclean leper's house
With the scent of costliest nard.

(Oscar Wilde, THE BALLAD OF READING GAOL)

Oscar Wilde is here referring to the incident at Simon the leper's house:

> *. . . as he [Christ] sat at meat, there came a woman having an alabaster box*
> *of ointment of spikenard very precious; and she brake the box, and poured it*
> *on his head.*

(MARK 14: 3)

The woman—she is not identified—was criticised by some of the company for her extravagance but hotly defended by Christ who was anticipating his imminent death:

> *Let her alone; why trouble ye her? She hath wrought a good work on me. For*
> *ye have the poor with you always, and whensoever ye will ye may do them*
> *good; but me ye have not always . . . she is come aforehand to anoint my*
> *body to the burying.*

(MARK 14: 6–8)

Jesus was anointed with spikenard on another occasion too, in Bethany, in the company of the newly resurrected Lazarus, Judas Iscariot, Mary and her sister Martha:

> *Then took Mary a pound of ointment of spikenard, very costly, and*
> *anointed the feet of Jesus, and wiped his feet with her hair: and the house*
> *was filled with the odour of the ointment.*

(JOHN 12: 3)

The hypocritical Judas complained of the waste of such a valuable substance but Jesus replied as before.

This ointment of spikenard must have been Mary's most treasured possession. Important in the sensual context of the bedroom (it is referred to in the SONG OF SOLOMON) as well as in religious ritual in the form of incense, the scent is somewhere between patchouli and valerian, to which it is related. All parts of the plant contain an aromatic essential oil which, though pure in Mary's precious salve, was sometimes mixed with other ingredients to make cosmetics and medicines. Perfumes and oils were commonly used in eastern countries and formed an indispensable part of the toilet of the wealthy—or, perhaps in the case of the 'woman who was a sinner' (LUKE 7: 37–38) of women with a professional interest in sensuality.

Boxes to contain these ointments were often made of wood and ivory, intricately carved, and many made of alabaster were found by Layard in the ruins of Nineveh. Frequently these containers had to be broken in order to release the contents, as in the case of the woman at Simon the leper's house. Spikenard, sometimes called Indian nard, or 'spike' would have been imported into the Holy Land, as it is a native of Nepal and other parts of the Himalayas from whence it was introduced into India. It used to be quite important medicinally, but is now almost obsolete. Its properties are similar to those of the common valerian which is still used for nervous problems, being sedative and anti-spasmodic.

Both of these plants are easy to grow in normal garden conditions, and it is interesting to experiment with their unusual aromas. Spikenard regained popularity in the 17th century and it appears in oriental-type pot-pourri recipes. Johnson, in his 1633 edition of Gerard's HERBALL, recommends it as being:

> *good to cause haire to grow on the eye lids of such as want it, and good to be strewed upon any part of the body that abounds with superfluous moisture, to dry it up.*

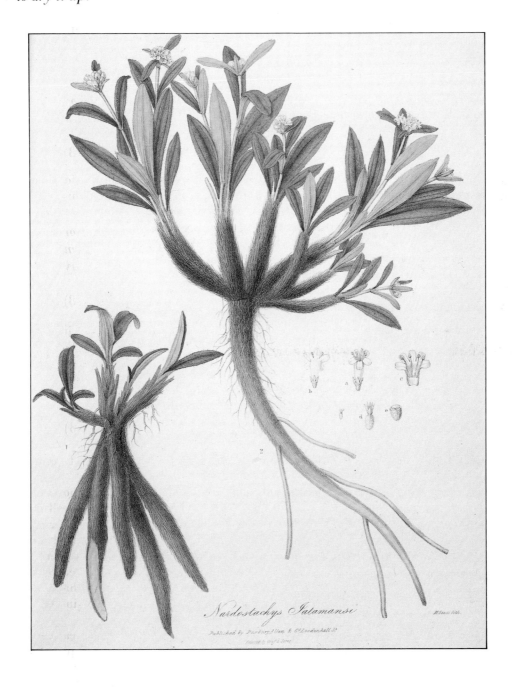

Nardostachys Jatamansi

(VALERIAN FAMILY—*VALERIANACEAE*)

133

SYCAMINE SYCOMORE

Morus nigra   *Ficus sycomorus*

*And the Lord said, If ye had faith as a grain of mustard seed, ye might say
unto this* sycamine *tree, Be thou plucked up by the root, and be thou planted
in the sea; and it should obey you.*

(LUKE 17: 6)

By common consent scholars are agreed that Luke is probably referring here to the
black mulberry, and later, in 19: 4, to the sycomore fig: 'And he ran before, and
climbed up into a *sycomore* tree to see him: for he was to pass that way.' And to confuse
matters further, the mulberry of 2 SAMUEL 5: 23–24:

> *. . . fetch a compass behind them, and come upon them over against the*
> mulberry *trees. And let it be, when thou hearest the sound of a gong in the*
> tops of the mulberry *trees, that then thou shalt bestir thyself . . .*

is not *Morus nigra*, but a tree not yet positively identified. The *New English* Bible gives
'aspen'.

It is clear from the works of early Greek and Roman writers that the mulberry tree
used to be an important tree of cultivation, and so it continued in Europe throughout the
Middle Ages until relatively recently. The fruit was a favourite of the Romans and they
probably introduced *Morus nigra* into Britain where it grows well in the South. James I
encouraged planting at the beginning of the 17th century in the hope of encouraging the
silk industry but this was unsuccessful, mainly because the black mulberry was mistakenly
planted instead of the white mulberry of China (*Morus alba*) which is the species on which
the silkworm thrives. In England, however, as a result, there are still many old mulberry
trees, though the fruit is a neglected delicacy. It is a tricky one to market as it bruises
easily, and stains deeply with its dark purple juice. If you take a branch from a mulberry
tree it will grow—slowly. It is late to bud and won't venture a leaf until all danger of
frost is over:

> *. . . observe the mulberry tree, when it begins to put forth and open the leaves
> (be it earlier or later), bring your oranges, &c. boldly out of the conservatory;
> 'tis your only season to transplant and remove them.*
> <div align="center">(<i>John Evelyn,</i> KALENDARIUM HORTENSE, <i>1664</i>)</div>

You can use mulberries like blackberries, in ice-creams, sorbets, tarts, summer puddings,
jams, jellies, wine, etc., and the fruit has medicinal value too, being slightly laxative and
expectorant. It is sweet and acidulous and contains malic and citric acids and pectin.
Here is some gynaecological advice from Culpeper:

> *A branch of the tree taken when the moon is at the full, and bound to the
> wrists of a woman's arm, whose courses come down too much, doth stay them
> in a short space.*
> (COMPLETE HERBAL AND ENGLISH PHYSICIAN)

The sycomore fig, or Egyptian mulberry, is related to *Ficus carica*, though it is a much larger tree whose light porous wood has been exploited in building work. The fruit is inferior to the true fig and less sweet, but it crops several times a year and has been of considerable food value to the poor. It bears the fruit in clusters which spring prolifically from the main stem.

> *There issueth foorth of the barke of this tree . . . a liquor, which being taken up with a spunge, or a little wooll, is dried . . . this mollifieth, closeth wounds togither, and dissolveth grosse humors.*
>
> (*Gerard's* HERBALL, *1597*)

The Mulberry Tree.

Publish'd Jan.r 1.1776 by A. Hunter M.D. as the Act directs   John Miller del et Sculp.

(MULBERRY FAMILY—*MORACEAE*)

TARE

(Darnel) *Lolium temulentum*

The kingdom of heaven is likened unto a man which sowed good seed in his field: But while men slept, his enemy came and sowed tares *among that wheat, and went his way. But when the blade was sprung up, and brought forth fruit, then appeared the* tares *also . . .*

(MATTHEW 13: 24–26)

The tare of the parable is the noxious weed, darnel (*Lolium temulentum*) which grows among wheat. Forsskal, writing in the 18th century, observes that 'the reapers do not separate the plant; but after the threshing, they reject the seeds by means of a van or sieve.'[16] Other travellers mention that the plant is gathered by hand, along with the wheat, and bound up in separate bundles and this is what happened in the parable.

Let both grow together until the harvest: and in the time of harvest I will say to the reapers, Gather ye together first the tares, *and bind them in bundles to burn them: but gather the wheat into my barn.*

(13: 30)

Obviously the darnel could not be properly distinguished from the wheat until mature.

The seeds of the tare are poisonous to men and animals, though some people believe that the ill-effects are caused by a fungus, like the ergot which attacks rye. Dizziness, nausea, vomiting and diarrhoea are the symptoms and the French call it *ivraie*, from *ivre* (drunkenness).

The new bread wherein Darnell is, eaten hot, causeth drunkennes: in like maner doth beere or ale wherein the seede is fallen, or put into the mault . . . Darnell hurteth the eies and maketh them dim, if it happen in corne either for bread or drinke.

(*Gerard's* HERBALL, *1597*)

Culpeper calls it 'a malicious part of sullen Saturn' but suggests that:

A decoction thereof made with water and honey, and the places bathed therewith, is profitable for the sciatica.

It is clear not only from the parable but from reports in more recent times that it was not unknown for seeds of this 'among the hurtfull weeds, the first,' to have been maliciously sown amongst the wheat in order to spoil the crop.

It was suggested at one time that the *fitches* of ISAIAH (28: 25 and 27) could have been tares of some kind—the *New English* Bible gives dill, but it is much more likely that they were the black, aromatic seeds of *Nigella sativa*, a type of cummin which is used in the east for flavouring and sprinkling on bread like sesame.

When he hath made plain the face thereof, doth he not cast abroad the fitches, *and scatter cummin . . .?*

(ISAIAH 28: 25)

(GRASS FAMILY—*GRAMINEAE*)

D.Blair F.L.S. ad nat. del. et lith.

M&N Hanhart imp.

LOLIUM TEMULENTUM, *Linn.*

THISTLES & THORNS

One of the inconveniences of the vegetable thickets is, that it is difficult to remain in them, seeing that nine-tenths of the trees and plants are armed with inexorable thorns, which suffer only an unquiet enjoyment of the shadow which is so constantly desirable, from the precaution necessary to guard against them.

So wrote one early 19th century traveller, Denon, and it is no wonder then that among so many kinds of thorny plants there are problems identifying the twenty or so mentioned in the scriptures. There are more than 70 such plants growing in Israel, and it is unlikely that people in Bible times could distinguish between say one thistle and another any more than most of us could today. And so these Hebrew words have been variously and erroneously mistranslated over the centuries. It would probably be more accurate simply to refer to them as thorns, or thistles, or briers rather than to try to identify specific plants.

. . . Because thou hast hearkened unto the voice of thy wife, and hast eaten of the tree, of which I commanded thee, saying, Thou shalt not eat of it: cursed is the ground for thy sake; in sorrow shalt thou eat of it all the days of thy life; Thorns also and thistles shall it bring forth to thee; and thou shalt eat the herb of the field.

(GENESIS 3: 17–18)

Thorns and thistles are generally used metaphorically, to emphasise worthlessness—'Let thistles grow instead of wheat, and cockle instead of barley. The words of Job are ended' (JOB 31: 40)—and they represent pain or evil, desolation, destruction and misery. They did have their practical uses however, and provided rough animal fodder and fuel for the fire:

'*For as the crackling of thorns under a pot, so is the laughter of the fool.*'

(ECCLESIASTES 7: 6)

But in general they were troublesome weeds, thistles such as *Silybum marianum* (Daisy family—*Compositae*) being one of the more common. This is Our Lady's Thistle or Milk Thistle, and tradition tells that the milk-white veins of its leaves originated from some of the Virgin's milk which fell on one of the plants. It was probably the 'thorn' of the parable of the sower too, growing prolifically as it does in the Holy Land at the edges of the corn fields suffocating the young grain.

Disarmed of its prickles and boiled, it is worthy of esteem, and thought to be a great breeder of milk, and proper diet for women who are nurses,

wrote John Evelyn, and hardy people also eat the heads like artichokes. It was believed to counteract melancholy, to ward off disease and to remove obstructions of the liver and spleen. *Silybum marianum* is a handsome plant too, worthy of a place in the garden.

Several varieties of thorn could have been used to plait the crown which was used to mock Christ, and Christian tradition has accepted one which is as likely as any of the others—*Ziziphus spina-christi* (Buckthorn family—*Rhamnaceae*). But crowns of *Calicotome villosa* (Pea family—*Leguminosae*), which also grows near Jerusalem, are plaited and sold to pilgrims there, and also the less cruel *Sarcopoterium spinosum* (Rose family—*Rosaceae*).

Carduus marianus

I laid me down upon a bank
Where love lay sleeping.
I heard among the rushes bank
Weeping, Weeping.

Then I went to the heath & the wild.
To the thistles & thorns of the waste.
And they told me how they beguil'd,
Driven out, & compel'd to be chaste.

('*Poems from MSS,*' *William Blake, c. 1793*)

VINE

Vitis vinifera

Anyone looking for textual support in the Bible for a case for temperance or abstinence from wine will look in vain, for although the pernicious effects of over-indulgence are deplored, both the *Old* and *New Testaments* are pervaded with the most cheerful images of wine and vines, vineyards and viticulture and vintage celebrations. It was all started by Noah who:

> *began to be an husbandman, and he planted a vineyard: And he drank of the wine, and was drunken . . .*
>
> (GENESIS 9: 20–21)

And in Mosaic law the culture of the vine was a matter of the utmost importance. With the olive and the fig, the vine became an emblem of the land of Israel and signified happiness, prosperity, peace and security:

> *And Judah and Israel dwelt safely, every man under his* vine *and under his fig tree . . .*
>
> (1 KINGS 4: 25)

It appeared decoratively on murals, mosaics, pottery, furniture, tombstones, and coins—a symbol of abundance, and blessing. Abundant it certainly was in the land of Canaan, from whence the two spies brought home such an enormous bunch of grapes that they had to carry it between them on a pole (NUMBERS 13: 23). A bottle of Bethlehem wine was a present fit for a King.

> *And Jesse took an ass laden with bread, and a bottle of wine, and a kid, and sent them by David his son unto Saul.*
>
> (1 SAMUEL 16: 20)

But at the everyday domestic level too, wine was clearly used much more than it is today. Jacob's blessing to Judah in GENESIS 49: 11 symbolises abundance:

> *Binding his foal unto the* vine, *and his ass's colt unto the choice* vine; *he washed his garments in wine, and his clothes in the blood of grapes.*

Curiously, although it has been made in Israel since the very beginnings of wine-making, there is limited interest there in expanding the industry which Baron Edmond de Rothschild initiated on French lines at the end of the 19th century. Consumption is low, and the preference is for the sweet wines used in religious observance, for example when breaking the fast after Passover or on sabbath nights.

I am the true vine, and my Father is the husbandman. Every branch in me that beareth not fruit he taketh away: and every branch that beareth fruit, he purgeth it, that it may bring forth more fruit . . .

(JOHN 15: 1–2)

Christ here is identifying himself with the vine, and highlighting too the nature of the essentially agricultural life of the Bible which is so vividly presented there.

For stern and cautionary words however, look to PROVERBS 23: 31–33:

Look not thou upon the wine when it is red, when it giveth his colour in the cup, when it moveth itself aright. At the last it biteth like a serpent, and stingeth like an adder. Thine eyes shall behold strange women, and thine heart shall utter perverse things . . .

(GRAPE FAMILY—VITACEAE)

Vitis vinifera.

WHEAT

Triticum durum

EMMER

Triticum dicoccum

> *But the* wheat *and the* rie *were not smitten; for they were not grown up.*
>
> (EXODUS 9: 32)

This refers to the seventh plague of Egypt when hail destroyed the flax and barley. The wheat was saved because it takes so much longer to mature. Wheat was, as now, the chief agricultural crop in the Holy Land, predominantly the *durum* variety which produces the excellent flour which is used for pasta in Italy, and *emmer* which is translated as *rie* above. (Rye was not grown there, and its cultivation is mostly confined to the USSR and Scandinavia).

It is hardly surprising that 'wheat', or the generic 'corn' or 'bread', appears so frequently in the Bible, both literally and figuratively, because bread was, and is, the staff of life. There is still today a good deal of superstitious and religious feeling attached to it—even in the West where we mark our loaves, or hot cross buns, with a symbolic cross—though we are perhaps sometimes unaware of why we do it. In the East bread is regarded as a direct gift of God and it is important in religious theory and practice both among Christians and Jews.

Jewish dietary laws are explicit concerning the eating of leavened or unleavened bread. The Passover commemorates the Exodus of the Israelites from Egypt when they were given so little time to make preparations that they could not leaven the bread before baking it. So, strict Jews will not eat leavened bread during the eight days of the festival.

The earliest record of the rite of bread and wine in Christian worship is in A.D. 55 as recorded by St Paul, and since then the Eucharist has resulted in many a schism between the Churches.

Wheat appears in more Sybaritic context too:

> *Thy navel is like a round goblet, which wanteth not liquor; thy belly is like an heap of* wheat *set about with lilies.*
>
> (SONG OF SOLOMON 7: 2)

Parched corn is mentioned several times, sometimes coupled with bread, and this was prepared by heating nearly ripe wheat on an iron griddle, or by binding the ears of corn into wisps by roasting them.

> *And Jesse said unto David his son, Take now for thy brethren an ephah of this* parched corn, *and these ten loaves, and run to the camp to thy brethren.*
>
> (1 SAMUEL 17: 17)

The practice sounds similar to that of *graddan* which survived in the Western Isles of Scotland until about the 18th century, and which helped to preserve the wheat, as well as making it possible to free the grains of early varieties like emmer, which were tightly encased and could not be threshed. Eastern bread, although made from durum wheat, which is high in the gluten-forming protein which gives dough its maximum elasticity, is none the less flattish and only slightly leavened. It is used throughout the meal, and pitta bread (as we know *khubz* in the West) can be cut in half and the pocket filled with savoury meat or bean mixtures and salad. Other grains were used with or without wheat for bread-making, such as millet, and the loaves of the miracle with the two fishes were of barley.

(GRASS FAMILY—*GRAMINEAE*)

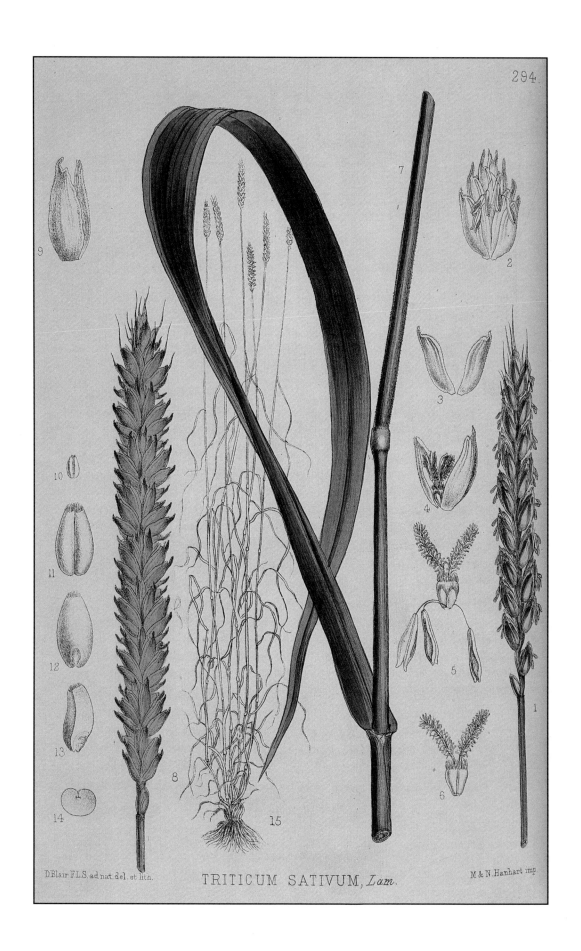

D.Blair F.L.S. ad nat. del. et lith.　　　TRITICUM SATIVUM, *Lam.*　　　M & N. Hanhart imp.

WILD GOURD

Citrullus colocynthis

*And one went out into the field to gather herbs, and found a wild vine, and
gathered thereof,* wild gourds *his lap full, and came and shred them into the
pot of pottage: for they knew them not. So they poured out for the men to eat.
And it came to pass, as they were eating of the pottage, that they cried out,
and said, O thou man of God, there is death in the pot. And they could not
eat thereof.*

(2 KINGS 4: 39–40)

The fruit which almost poisoned Elisha's young men is a kind of gourd, attractive and
inviting-looking, but intolerably bitter to the taste and a drastic purgative.

*Which operation of purging it worketh so violently, that it doth not onely
draw foorth flegme and choler marveilous speedily, and in very great quantity:
but oftentimes fetcheth foorth bloud and bloudie excrements, by shaving the
guts, and opening the endes of the meseraicall veines.*

Gerard's description (1597) of the action of *colocynthis* would make one wary, to put it
mildly, and his recommendation that 'the seed is very profitable to keepe and preserve
dead bodies with; especially if Aloes and Myrrhe be mixed with it,' hardly inspires
confidence in any positive powers.

The pottage was eaten none the less, without ill effects, having been tempered by the
prophet:

*. . . he said, Then bring meal. And he cast it into the pot; and he said, Pour
out for the people, that they may eat. And there was no harm in the pot.*

(2 KINGS 4: 41)

The drug consists of the dried pulp of the fruit, the best being the Turkish colocynth
which is imported from Cyprus and Syria. It is a powerful cathartic, extremely irritant,
and rarely used alone because of its drastic nature. In cases of poisoning opium is given
after emptying the stomach, and this is followed by stimulants and demulcent drinks. $1\frac{1}{2}$
teaspoons of the powder can be fatal—death in the pot indeed. But the fruits, broken up
into small pieces, make a good moth repellent.

It has been suggested that colocynthis—bitter apple or vine of the field as it is
sometimes called—was possibly the vine of DEUTERONOMY 32: 32:

For their vine *is of the* vine *of Sodom, and of the fields of Gomorrah: their
grapes are grapes of gall, their clusters are bitter . . .*

But this seems unlikely and *vine of sodom* would appear to be a symbolic concept rather
than an explicit term.

(PUMPKIN FAMILY—*CUCURBITACEAE*)

G. Spratt del et lithog

Printed by C. Hullmandel.

Cucumis Colocynthis.

WILLOW

Salix alba

By the rivers of Babylon, there we sat down, yea, we wept, when we remembered Zion. We hanged our harps upon the willows in the midst thereof. For there they that carried us away captive required of us a song; and they that wasted us required of us mirth, saying, Sing us one of the songs of Zion.

(PSALM 137: 1–3)

Willow generally implies grief and bitterness. Jilted lovers in Shakespeare's day wore garlands of willow, Desdemona sings the *Willow Song*, Ophelia drowns by a willow when she tries to hang her flowers on it. In fact, the willow of the Psalm was probably a poplar—but the association persists, and the weeping willow, native of the east, is *Salix babylonica*. This species is not a native of either Babylon or the Holy Land; that it is from China is clear from the well-loved willow pattern ware which is still so popular today.

Thus o'er our streams do eastern willows lean
In pensive guise; whose grief-inspiring shade
Love has to melancholy sacred made.

(*Delille*, L'HOMME DES CHAMPS)

The Willow does unquestionably appear in the Scriptures as in ISAIAH 44: 3–4:

For I will pour water upon him that is thirsty, and floods upon the dry ground: I will pour my spirit upon thy seed, and my blessing upon thine offspring: And they shall spring up as among the grass, as willows by the water courses.

As implied here, willows are easily propagated. Place fairly large cuttings in open ground between November and March, preferably in the moist situation that is natural to them, and they should root easily. There are many attractive varieties and they are valuable to the beekeeper for early pollen and nectar supplies. They grow fast too, (hence the Latin name from *salire*, to leap) and have many traditional uses—baskets, hoops, poles, ladders, and small casks, and more recently cricket bats and artificial limbs. You can whet knives on willow, tan leather and dye yarn a cinnamon colour and make paper with the cottony down that covers the seeds.

The tree is as bitter as its associations and contains a high percentage of tannin. Country people used to drink infusions of the bark against the ague, and the tonic and astringent properties of *Salix alba* are valuable in convalescence from acute disease, and in cases of worms, chronic diarrhoea and dysentery.

The leaves bruised and boiled in wine, and drank, stays the heat of lust in man or woman, and quite extinguishes it, if it be long used

writes Culpeper. Perhaps this was why it was popular with rejected lovers. Gerard's suggestion is more cheerful:

The greene boughes with the leaves may very well be brought into chambers, and set about the beds of those that be sicke of agues: for they do mightily coole the heate of the aire, which thing is a woonderfull refreshing to the sicke patients.

(*Gerard's* HERBALL, *1597*)

1263 Salix alba L.

(WILLOW FAMILY—SALICACEAE)

WORMWOOD

Artemisia

*And the third angel sounded, and there fell a great star from heaven, burning
as it were a lamp, and it fell upon the third part of the rivers, and upon the
fountains of waters; And the name of the star is called* Wormwood: *and the
third part of the waters became* wormwood; *and many men died of the waters,
because they were made bitter.*

(REVELATION 8: 10–11)

In 1986 there occurred in Russia, at the power plant at Chernobyl, the most disastrous-
ever nuclear accident, which resulted in death, devastation of the surrounding
countryside, and fearful contamination of soil, herbage and livestock for thousands of
miles around. More than a year later, radioactive levels were still worryingly high, even in
such remote parts as the Lake District of England and parts of Scotland, while the long-
term effects are still imponderable. From a linguistic point of view, one of the most
interesting things about the word 'Chernobyl' is that in Russian it refers to 'a large variety
of wormwood', *Artemisia vulgaris*, (and in Tver Region *Artemisia campestris* and *A.
scoparia*). For anyone familiar with the above passage and the surrounding text in
REVELATION it is impossible not to be overwhelmed by the force of the connection—or
even awesome coincidence.

Artemis, incidentally, was one of the great divinities of the Greeks. The Romans called
her Diana, and she was goddess of the moon, chastity and hunting. Although capable of
curing or alleviating human suffering, her arrows are frequently associated with disaster
or plague and particularly with the sudden death of women.

The plant has a nauseous smell and an extremely bitter taste:

He hath filled me with bitterness, he hath made me drunken with wormwood
. . . Remembering mine affliction and my misery, the wormwood *and the
gall.*

(LAMENTATIONS 3: 15, 19)

Sometimes it appears in company with hemlock or gall, but the plant's bitterness is
always stressed, and figuratively it signifies calamity—'but her end is bitter as wormwood'
(PROVERBS 5: 4). Probably the variety referred to in the Bible (and they all possess similar
properties) is *Artemisia herba-alba*, which grows profusely in the deserts of Israel.
Wormwood is still used as a vermifuge, and a bitter tea is still made of it by the Bedouin
in Sinai. In France, at the end of the 19th century, abuse of absinthe, the spirit made
from the essence of this plant, or rather from *Artemisia absinthium*, caused such abject
misery and degradation that its manufacture was prohibited in 1915. Degas immortalised
this social phenomenon in his painting of 1876, *The Absinthe Drinkers*.

The drug absinthium, which consists of the dried leaves and flowering tops, stimulates
the cerebral hemisphere and habitual use or large doses produce absinthism, which is
shown by restlessness, vomiting, vertigo, tremors and convulsions. Excessive drinking of
absinthe leads to even more pronounced and permanent deterioration of the mind than
that of ordinary alcoholism—stupor and appalling hallucinations. Nonetheless the herb
does have significant medicinal value, and is used as a tonic, an appetite stimulant, a
vermifuge, for stomach disorders and externally as a wash for diseases of the eye. 'The

common Wormwood ... is powerful against the gout and gravel,' says Culpeper and Gerard recommends it for 'them that are strangled with eating of mushrumes, or toad stooles, if it be drunke with vineger.'

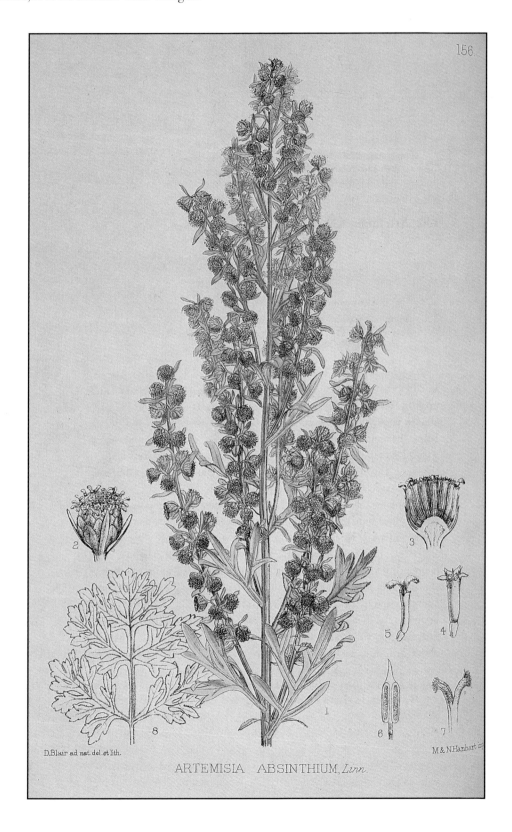

ARTEMISIA ABSINTHIUM, *Linn.*

D.Blair ad nat. del. et lith.

M & N.Hanhart

(DAISY FAMILY—*COMPOSITAE*)

NOTES

1. This medieval recipe is quoted in FOOD AND DRINK IN BRITAIN, © **Anne Wilson.**
2. Ibid.
3. Recipe from THE COOK AND HOUSEWIFE'S MANUAL by Meg Dods (1826).
4. Recipe from THE SHOESTRING GOURMET (1986) by Wilma Paterson.
5. Ibid.
6. Jackson is quoted in THE NATURAL HISTORY OF THE BIBLE by Thaddeus Mason Harris, 1824.
7. Recipe from THE SHOESTRING GOURMET (1986) by Wilma Paterson.
8. Ibid.
9. Recipe from ENCICLOPEDIA DELLE ERBE E DELLE PIANTE MEDICINALI, Tina Cecchini.
10. From Biddulph's COLLECTION OF VOYAGES AND TRAVELS, Library of the Earl of Oxford.
11. John Parkinson was an important 17th century herbalist, author of PARADISI IN SOLE, PARADISUS TERRISTRIS.
12. From ENCICLOPEDIA DELLE ERBE E DELLE PIANTE MEDICINALI, Tina Cecchini.
13. Ibid.
14. Recipe from BOOK OF COCKTAILS, 1927.
15. Recipe from THE SHOESTRING GOURMET (1986) by Wilma Paterson.
16. Excerpt of Forsskal in Thaddeus Mason Harris, THE NATURAL HISTORY OF THE BIBLE, 1824.

PICTURE SOURCES

FLORA GRAECA : Sibthorp (1819)
FLORA DANICA : G. C. OEDER (1776)
FLORA LONDINENSIS, enlarged by HOOKER (1835)
SYLVA, or A DISCOURSE OF FOREST TREES : JOHN EVELYN (1776)
FLORA MEDICA : GEORGE SPRATT (1829)
MEDICINAL PLANTS : BENTLEY & TRIMEN (1880)
TRAITE DES ARBRES : DUHAMEL (1755)
SPECIES GRAMINUM : TRINIUS (1828)
ICONES FLORAE GERMANICAE ET HELVETICAE : REICHENBACH (1827)
LILIACEES : REDOUTE (1824)
ILLUSTRATIONS OF THE BOTANY AND OTHER BRANCHES OF THE
    NATURAL HISTORY OF THE HIMALAYAN MOUNTAINS:
    J. FORBES ROYLE (1839)
ASIA : DAPPER (1688)
ILLUSTRATIONS OF INDIAN BOTANY : ROBERT WIGHT (1840)

SELECTED BIBLIOGRAPHY

Beeton, Isabella, BOOK OF HOUSEHOLD MANAGEMENT (London 1861)

Cecchini, Tina, ENCICLOPEDIA DELLE ERBE E DELLE PIANTE MEDICINALI (Milano 1981)

Cobbett, William, COTTAGE ECONOMY (London 1850)

Culpeper, Nicholas, COMPLETE HERBAL AND ENGLISH PHYSICIAN (Manchester 1826)

Dods, Meg (C. I. Johnstone) THE COOK AND HOUSEWIFE'S MANUAL (Edinburgh 1826)

Evelyn, John, ACETARIA, A DISCOURSE OF SALLETS (London 1699)

Evelyn, John, SYLVA, or A DISCOURSE OF FOREST-TREES (London 1664)

Gerard, John, THE HERBALL OR GENERAL HISTORIE OF PLANTS (London 1597)

Gerard, John, THE HERBALL, ENLARGED AND AMENDED BY THOMAS JOHNSON (London 1633)

Grieve, Mrs M., A MODERN HERBAL (London 1976)

Grigson, Geoffrey, THE ENGLISHMAN'S FLORA (London 1958)

Harris, Thaddeus Mason, THE NATURAL HISTORY OF THE BIBLE (London 1824)

Hastings, James, (Editor) A DICTIONARY OF THE BIBLE (Edinburgh 1898)

Lane, Edward William, AN ACCOUNT OF THE MANNERS AND CUSTOMS OF THE MODERN EGYPTIANS (London 1860, fifth edition)

M. F. M., SCRIPTURE MANNERS AND CUSTOMS (London 1949)

Ovid, METAMORPHOSES (London 1955)

Parkinson, John, PARADISI IN SOLE, PARADISUS TERRESTRIS (London 1629)

Paterson, Wilma, THE SHOESTRING GOURMET (Edinburgh 1986)

Phillips, Henry, SYLVA FLORIFERA (London 1823)

Roden, Claudia, A BOOK OF MIDDLE EASTERN FOOD (London 1968)

Temple, Augusta A., FLOWERS AND TREES OF PALESTINE (London 1929)

Turner, William, A NEW HERBALL (London 1551)

Wilson, C. Anne, FOOD AND DRINK IN BRITAIN (London 1973)

Zohary, Michael, PLANTS OF THE BIBLE (Cambridge 1982)

INDEX